W9-CAJ-369

Use Case Driven Object Modeling with UML

The Addison-Wesley Object Technology Series

Grady Booch, Ivar Jacobson, and James Rumbaugh, Series Editors

For more information check out the series web site [http://www.awl.com /cseng/otseries/] as well as the pages on each book [http://www.awl.com/cseng/I-S-B-N/] (I-S-B-N represents the actual ISBN, including dashes).

David Bellin and Susan Suchman Simone, *The CRC Card Book*, ISBN 0-201-89535-8

Grady Booch, *Object Solutions: Managing the Object-Oriented Project*, ISBN 0-8053-0594-7

Grady Booch, *Object-Oriented Analysis and Design with Applications, Second Edition*, ISBN 0-8053-5340-2

Grady Booch, James Rumbaugh, and Ivar Jacobson, *The Unified Modeling Language User Guide*, ISBN 0-201-57168-4

Don Box, *Essential COM*, ISBN 0-201-63446-5

Don Box, Keith Brown, Tim Ewald, and Chris Sells, *Effective COM: 50 Ways to Improve Your COM and MTS-based Applications*, ISBN 0-201-37968-6

Alistair Cockburn, *Surviving Object-Oriented Projects: A Manager's Guide*, ISBN 0-201-49834-0

Dave Collins, *Designing Object-Oriented User Interfaces*, ISBN 0-8053-5350-X

Bruce Powel Douglass, *Doing Hard Time: Designing and Implementing Embedded Systems with UML*, ISBN 0-201-49837-5

Bruce Powel Douglass, *Real-Time UML: Developing Efficient Objects for Embedded Systems*, ISBN 0-201-32579-9

Desmond F. D'Souza and Alan Cameron Wills, *Objects, Components, and Frameworks with UML: The Catalysis Approach*, ISBN 0-201-31012-0

Martin Fowler, *Analysis Patterns: Reusable Object Models*, ISBN 0-201-89542-0

Martin Fowler, *Refactoring: Improving the Design of Existing Code*, ISBN 0-201-48567-2

Martin Fowler with Kendall Scott, *UML Distilled: Applying the Standard Object Modeling Language*, ISBN 0-201-32563-2

Peter Heinckiens, *Building Scalable Database Applications: Object-Oriented Design, Architectures, and Implementations*, ISBN 0-201-31013-9

Ivar Jacobson, Grady Booch, and James Rumbaugh, *The Unified Software Development Process*, ISBN 0-201-57169-2

Ivar Jacobson, Magnus Christerson, Patrik Jonsson, and Gunnar Overgaard, *Object-Oriented Software Engineering: A Use Case Driven Approach*, ISBN 0-201-54435-0

Ivar Jacobson, Maria Ericsson, and Agneta Jacobson, *The Object Advantage: Business Process Reengineering with Object Technology,* ISBN 0-201-42289-1

Ivar Jacobson, Martin Griss, and Patrik Jonsson, *Software Reuse: Architecture, Process and Organization for Business Success,* ISBN 0-201-92476-5

David Jordan, *C++ Object Databases: Programming with the ODMG Standard*, ISBN 0-201-63488-0

Philippe Kruchten, *The Rational Unified Process: An Introduction,* ISBN 0-201-60459-0

Wilf LaLonde, *Discovering Smalltalk*, ISBN 0-8053-2720-7

Lockheed Martin Advanced Concepts Center and Rational Software Corporation, *Succeeding with the Booch and OMT Methods: A Practical Approach*, ISBN 0-8053-2279-5

Thomas Mowbray and William Ruh, *Inside CORBA: Distributed Object Standards and Applications*, ISBN 0-201-89540-4

Bernd Oestereich, *Developing Software with UML: Object-Oriented Analysis and Design in Practice*, ISBN 0-201-39826-5

Ira Pohl, *Object-Oriented Programming Using C++, Second Edition,* ISBN 0-201-89550-1

Rob Pooley and Perdita Stevens, *Using UML: Software Engineering with Objects and Components*, ISBN 0-201-36067-5

Terry Quatrani, *Visual Modeling with Rational Rose and UML*, ISBN 0-201-31016-3

Brent E. Rector and Chris Sells, *ATL Internals*, ISBN 0-201-69589-8

Doug Rosenberg with Kendall Scott, *Use Case Driven Object Modeling with UML: A Practical Approach*, ISBN 0-201-43289-7

Walker Royce, *Software Project Management: A Unified Framework,* ISBN 0-201-30958-0

William Ruh, Thomas Herron, and Paul Klinker, *IIOP Complete: Middleware Interoperability and Distributed Object Standards,* ISBN 0-201-37925-2

James Rumbaugh, Ivar Jacobson, and Grady Booch, *The Unified Modeling Language Reference Manual*, ISBN 0-201-30998-X

Geri Schneider and Jason P. Winters, *Applying Use Cases: A Practical Guide*, ISBN 0-201-30981-5

Yen-Ping Shan and Ralph H. Earle, *Enterprise Computing with Objects: From Client/Server Environments to the Internet,* ISBN 0-201-32566-7

David N. Smith, *IBM Smalltalk: The Language*, ISBN 0-8053-0908-X

Daniel Tkach, Walter Fang, and Andrew So, *Visual Modeling Technique: Object Technology Using Visual Programming,* ISBN 0-8053-2574-3

Daniel Tkach and Richard Puttick, *Object Technology in Application Development, Second Edition*, ISBN 0-201-49833-2

Jos Warmer and Anneke Kleppe, *The Object Constraint Language: Precise Modeling with UML*, ISBN 0-201-37940-6

Use Case Driven Object Modeling with UML

A Practical Approach

Doug Rosenberg

with

Kendall Scott

ADDISON-WESLEY

An imprint of Addison Wesley Longman, Inc.

Reading, Massachusetts • Harlow, England • Menlo Park, California
Berkeley, California • Don Mills, Ontario • Sydney
Bonn • Amsterdam • Tokyo • Mexico City

Many of the designations used by manufacturers and sellers to distinguish their products are claimed as trademarks. Where those designations appear in this book, and Addison Wesley Longman, Inc., was aware of a trademark claim, the designations have been printed in initial capital letters or all capital letters.

The authors and publisher have taken care in preparation of this book, but make no expressed or implied warranty of any kind and assume no responsibility for errors or omissions. No liability is assumed for incidental or consequential damages in connection with or arising out of the use of the information or programs contained herein.

The publisher offers discounts on this book when ordered in quantity for special sales. For more information, please contact:

AWL Direct Sales
Addison Wesley Longman, Inc.
One Jacob Way
Reading, Massachusetts 01867
(781) 944-3700

Visit AW on the Web: **www.awl.com/cseng/**

Library of Congress Cataloging-in-Publication Data

Rosenberg, Doug.
    Use case driven object modeling with UML : a practical approach /
Doug Rosenberg with Kendall Scott.
        p.   cm. — (Addison-Wesley object technology series)
    Includes bibliographical references and index.
    ISBN 0-201-43289-7 (alk. paper)
    1. Object-oriented methods (Computer science)   2. UML (Computer science)   3. Use cases (Systems engineering)   I. Scott, Kendall.
II. Title   III. Series
QA76.9.O35R66   1999
005.1'17—dc21   99-12043
                                                         CIP

Copyright © 1999 by Addison Wesley Longman, Inc.

All rights reserved. No part of this publication may be reproduced, stored in a retrieval system, or transmitted, in any form or by any means, electronic, mechanical, photocopying, recording, or otherwise, without the prior written consent of the publisher. Printed in the United States of America. Published simultaneously in Canada.

Executive Editor: J. Carter Shanklin
Project Editor: Krysia Bebick
Editorial Assistant: Kristin Erickson
Project Manager: Sarah Weaver
Copyeditor: Arlene Richman
Composition: Kim Arney
Index: Kendall Scott
Cover Design: Simone Payment

Text printed on recycled and acid-free paper.

ISBN 0-201-43289-7

2 3 4 5 6 7   CRS   02 01 00 99

2nd Printing   June 1999

Contents

Figures ix

Analysis Paralysis Alerts xi

Top 10 Lists xiii

Preface xv

Chapter 1: The ICONIX Unified Object Modeling Approach 1
    Background 3
    Introduction to the Approach 5
    Thoughts on Methodology 8
    Process Fundamentals 9
    The Approach in a Nutshell 11

Chapter 2: Domain Modeling 15
    Discover Classes 17
    Build Generalization Relationships 21
    Build Associations Between Classes 23
    Develop Association Classes 26
    Mine Your Legacy Documentation for
    Domain Classes 27
    Draw an Analysis-Level Class Diagram 32
    Continue to Iterate and Refine 33

Chapter 3: Use Case Modeling 37
    Use Cases, Actors, and Use Case Diagrams 38
    Analysis-Level and Design-Level Use Cases 40

Writing Use Cases 40
    Working Inward from a GUI to Identify Use Cases 41
    Mining Your Legacy User Manuals for Use Cases 45
    Refining Use Cases 46
Basic and Alternate Courses of Action 47
Factoring Out Commonality in Usage 49
    Constructs from the UML and OML 49
    Back to Our Example 51
Use Case Packages 55
Use Cases and Requirements 56
Wrapping Up Use Case Modeling 57

Chapter 4: Robustness Analysis 61
Key Roles of Robustness Analysis 63
    Sanity Check 63
    Completeness Check 64
    Object Identification 65
    Preliminary Design 65
More About Robustness Analysis Object Types 66
Performing Robustness Analysis 67
Updating Your Domain (Static) Model 74
Wrapping Up Robustness Analysis 78

Chapter 5: Interaction Modeling 81
Goals of Interaction Modeling 82
Sequence Diagrams 84
Getting Started 85
Putting Methods on Classes 93
Examples 96
Updating Your Static Model 100
    Finalizing Attributes and Methods 101
    Ensuring Quality 102
    Adding Infrastructure 103
    Patternizing Your Design 104
    Back to the Example 104
Completing Interaction Modeling 105

Chapter 6: Collaboration and State Modeling 109

    When Do We Need Collaboration Diagrams? 110

    State Diagrams. 113

    How Many State Diagrams Do We Need? 113

    Activity Diagrams. 116

    Extending Interaction Modeling. 117

Chapter 7: Addressing Requirements 121

    What Is a Requirement? 122

    The Nature of Requirements, Use Cases,
    and Functions 123

    Requirements Traceability. 126

    Extending a Visual Modeling Tool
    to Support Requirements. 128

    Requirements and the ICONIX Approach 129

    Getting Ready to Code. 130

Chapter 8: Implementation 135

    Project Staffing Issues. 136

    Project Management. 137

    Revisiting the Static Model 138

    Allocating Classes to Components. 139

    Code Headers 139

    Testing 142

    Metrics 143

    Tracking Use Case Driven Development 146

    Wrapping Up. 147

Appendix: "Uses" vs. "Extends" 149

Bibliography 157

Index 159

Figures

Figure 1-1 The ICONIX Unified Object Modeling Approach 1
Figure 1-2 The ICONIX Approach, Showing
Three Amigos' Contributions 7
Figure 1-3 Requirements Analysis 11
Figure 1-4 Analysis and Preliminary Design 12
Figure 1-5 Design 13
Figure 1-6 Implementation 13

Figure 2-1 Working Outward from Data Requirements 16
Figure 2-2 Nouns in Example System Requirements 18
Figure 2-3 First Set of Candidate Classes for Example System 18
Figure 2-4 Refined Set of Candidate Classes 19
Figure 2-5 Candidate Classes After Further Refinement 21
Figure 2-6 Class Notations 21
Figure 2-7 Generalization of Trade Class 22
Figure 2-8 Generalization of Investment Class 23
Figure 2-9 Candidate Associations 24
Figure 2-10 Association Notation 25
Figure 2-11 Aggregation 26
Figure 2-12 Association Class 27
Figure 2-13 Oversize Trade Class, Ripe for Factoring 28
Figure 2-14 Helper Classes (Part 1) 29
Figure 2-15 Oversize Investment Class, Ripe for Factoring 30
Figure 2-16 Helper Classes (Part 2) 31
Figure 2-17 Analysis-Level Class Diagram 32
Figure 2-18 Requirements Analysis Checkpoint 1 34

Figure 3-1 Working Inward From User Requirements 38
Figure 3-2 Use Case Diagram 39
Figure 3-3 Sample Screen Mockup 42
Figure 3-4 Windows Navigation Diagram Elements 43
Figure 3-5 Sample Windows Navigation Diagram 43

Figure 3-6   Linking Files to Use Cases Within Rational Rose 44
Figure 3-7   Use Case Factoring 52
Figure 3-8   Use Case Diagram for Example System 55
Figure 3-9   Package Diagram for Example System 56
Figure 3-10   Requirements Analysis Checkpoint 2 58
Figure 3-11   Analysis and Preliminary Design Checkpoint 1 59

Figure 4-1   What vs. How 62
Figure 4-2   Robustness Diagram Symbols 68
Figure 4-3   Robustness Diagram Rules 69
Figure 4-4   Use Cases for Example System 70
Figure 4-5   Robustness Diagram for Perform Order Entry Use Case 72
Figure 4-6   Robustness Diagram for Enter Buy Trade Use Case 73
Figure 4-7   Updating the Domain Model as Part of Robustness Analysis . . 75
Figure 4-8   Robustness Model–Static Model Feedback Loop 76
Figure 4-9   Static Model After Robustness Analysis (Part 1) 77
Figure 4-10   Static Model After Robustness Analysis (Part 2) 78
Figure 4-11   Analysis and Preliminary Design Checkpoint 2 79

Figure 5-1   Sequence Diagram Elements 85
Figure 5-2   Building a Sequence Diagram 87
Figure 5-3   Starting the Sequence Diagram (Step 1) 88
Figure 5-4   Adding Entity Objects (Step 2) 90
Figure 5-5   Adding Actors and Boundary Objects (Step 3) 91
Figure 5-6   CRC Card 95
Figure 5-7   Sequence Diagram for Enter Buy Trade Use Case 98
Figure 5-8   Sequence Diagram for Perform Order Entry Use Case 99
Figure 5-9   Updating Your Static Model, Again 101
Figure 5-10   Design-Level Class Diagram 105
Figure 5-11   Design Checkpoint 1 106

Figure 6-1   Collaboration Diagram 112
Figure 6-2   State Diagram 115
Figure 6-3   Design Checkpoint 2 118

Figure 7-1   Billy Bob's Behavior 124
Figure 7-2   Objects Associated with Billy Bob 125
Figure 7-3   Requirements Tab Within Rational Rose 129
Figure 7-4   Traceability 130
Figure 7-5   Requirements Analysis Checkpoint 3 131
Figure 7-6   Design Checkpoint 2 132

Figure 8-1   Component Diagram 139
Figure 8-2   Design-Level Class Diagram Excerpt 140
Figure 8-3   Enter Buy Trade Sequence Diagram with Headers 141
Figure 8-4   How Our Example System Performed 145
Figure 8-5   Tracking Our Example System's Diagrams 147
Figure 8-6   Implementation Checkpoint 1 147

Analysis Paralysis Alerts

ALERT! Don't get bogged down in grammatical inspection. 20

ALERT! Don't address multiplicity too early in the project. 24

ALERT! Don't worry about aggregation and composition
until detailed design. 26

ALERT! Don't try to write use cases until you know what
the users will actually be doing. 46

ALERT! Don't spend weeks building elaborate, elegant use
case models that you can't design from. 50

ALERT! Don't spin your wheels worrying about whether
to use includes, extends, and/or uses. 50

ALERT! Don't waste time with long and involved use
case templates. 51

ALERT! Don't try to do detailed design on robustness diagrams. 66

ALERT! Don't waste time perfecting your robustness diagrams
as your design evolves. 76

ALERT! Don't try to allocate behavior among objects
before you have a good idea what the objects are. 83

ALERT! Don't start drawing a sequence diagram before you've
completed the associated robustness diagram. 85

ALERT! Don't focus on get and set methods instead of focusing
on real methods. 101

ALERT! Don't do state diagrams for objects with two states. 110

ALERT! Don't model what you don't really need to model. 114

ALERT! Don't do state diagrams just because you can. 114

Top 10 Lists

Top 10 Domain Modeling Errors 34

Top 10 Mistakes to Avoid When Writing Use Cases 60

Top 10 Benefits of Robustness Analysis 79

Top 10 Points to Remember When Drawing Sequence Diagrams 107

Top 10 Ways to Catch a Case of Analysis Paralysis. 119

Top 10 Things You Shall Remember About Requirements. 133

Top 10 Ways to Mess Up Your Project Despite Doing Good OOA&D 148

Preface

We've written this book with the following presumptions about you, the reader:

- You'd like to write some code, eventually, but you've decided that first you're going to do good, thorough OO analysis and design, expressed in the UML.
- You'd like to write this code during the useful life of your project.
- You'd like this code to meet the requirements of your users (in other words, you'd like to be use case driven in your modeling efforts).
- You'd like a solid, maintainable, resilient OO architecture within which to organize your code.

This book is designed to help you get from point A (use cases) to point B (code) in the most efficient manner possible, using an approach that's been proven to work on a wide variety of projects. In short, I'm aiming to answer the following question:

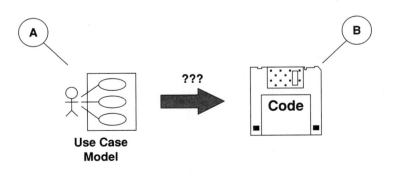

How do we get from use cases to code?

Theory vs. Practice

The difference between theory and practice is that, in theory, there is no difference between theory and practice.

More specifically: the reason this book is subtitled *A Practical Approach* is that the three amigos—Grady Booch, Jim Rumbaugh, and Ivar Jacobson—write what amounts to OO theory, even in the new (as I write this) *Unified Modeling Language User Guide*.

Allow me to explain.

The cold, hard reality of the world of software development is that there is simply never enough time for modeling. This means that even though the UML generally provides at least three different ways to describe a given aspect of development, project schedules usually make it impractical to use more than one, let alone all three. To make things worse, just trying to decide whether to use this UML technique or that one can be incredibly time-consuming.

Therefore, I offer a simplified view that makes no attempt to cover everything that the UML offers. Some of the more esoteric topics that I don't talk about, or mention but don't discuss in detail, are activity diagrams, deployment diagrams, use case collaborations, multilevel statecharts, and types and roles. Rather, I'm presenting a *streamlined* approach to software development that includes a minimal set of diagrams and techniques that you can use to get from use cases to code *quickly* and *efficiently*. You can always elect to use other aspects of the UML if you find them helpful; my approach is flexible and open.

In a couple of cases, where they make the job easier, I use extensions to standard UML. I make no apologies for doing this: the UML was designed to *be* extensible, and rightly so. The extensions that I advocate in this book work—they save time and money, and yield good results as well. The positive results associated with my years of teaching experience, in connection with dozens of projects in a wide range of industries, support that last statement.

Organization of This Book

This book has eight chapters. Let's start with our desired destination (code, of course) and work backwards.

Before we can get to code, which I address in Chapter 8, *Implementation*, we need to have a complete set of classes with accompanying attributes and methods.

We have only enough information to make good decisions about which classes are responsible for which methods while we are drawing sequence diagrams (the subject of Chapter 5, *Interaction Modeling*). So, we need to do a sequence diagram for every use case. We will allocate methods to classes as we do this.

Before we can draw a sequence diagram for a use case, we need to have a pretty good idea what objects will be participating in that use case, and what functions the system will perform as a result of user actions. We get this information from robustness diagrams, which result from *Robustness Analysis* (Chapter 4). We will discover new objects and add attributes to classes as we draw robustness diagrams.

Before we draw a robustness diagram, though, we need to describe system usage in the context of the object model; in other words, we need to write use case text, following the guidelines I present in Chapter 3, *Use Case Modeling*. We also need to explicitly name our "boundary objects," which the "actors" will use to interface with our new system, and account for special cases of behavior. We will discover new objects as we do these things.

Before we can write use case text, we need to identify the main abstractions present in the problem domain. In other words, we need a domain model. Thus, Chapter 2: *Domain Modeling*.

Chapter 1 describes the overall approach. Chapter 6 discusses collaboration diagrams and state diagrams, which are optional within the approach. And Chapter 7 talks about how to deal with requirements throughout a project.

We've used a portfolio trading and accounting system as an example throughout the book. You can find the Rational Rose model for this example at **http://www.iconixsw.com/BookExample.html**.

We'd like to highlight two features that we think help make this book unique in the world of OO.

- "Top 10" lists appear at the end of each chapter after Chapter 1. These summarize the points I make within the preceding text in ways that I hope you will find handy for repeated reference.

- "Analysis paralysis" alerts are scattered throughout the main text. These highlight those points in a software development project at which it's all too easy to get bogged down in nonproductive activities.

I should also point out that this book is considerably more fun, not to mention funnier, than most OO books.

Acknowledgments

Although this book is written in my voice, it was actually written, for the most part, by Kendall Scott. This, of course, makes him completely responsible for anything you may not like about it, while I am completely responsible for everything else (that is, all of the *good* stuff).

If you've never had a book written for you in your voice (and you probably haven't), it's actually quite an interesting process, involving a lot of mumbling "Did I actually say that?" to yourself. My advice to you is, don't attempt it unless you happen to be working with a helluva good writer, like Kendall. (Hold your calls to Kendall, though— we had so much fun writing this book that we're now threatening to do another one.)

Most of this book was written by E-mail. A very fortunate thing happened early on in this process: we each discovered that the other guy had a similarly twisted sense of humor. Luckily, no other human will ever see the very long chain of mail messages that led up to the creation of this epic. (We learned one thing from the big Microsoft antitrust litigation, anyway.)

At any rate, we hope that whatever kind of bizarre and unique chemistry came about from this unholy alliance has resulted in a book that you will actually enjoy reading and find useful, all at the same time.

This book would, of course, never have happened had it not been for the work of the three amigos, and particularly for the work that Ivar Jacobson *et al.* did several years ago in Sweden, where they actually figured out this step-by-step approach to OOA&D. I sincerely hope that work doesn't get lost in the shuffle of "the new and improved way of doing business."

I'd like to thank the following reviewers:

- Perry Cole, of MCI WorldCom
- Steve Ash
- Jim Conallen, of Clarity
- Joel Erickson, of Litton Guidance and Control Systems

I'd also like to express my appreciation for the folks (you know who you are) who critiqued our work in progress during training workshops that I held around the country during the past year.

Next, thank you to the three "K's" at Addison-Wesley: Kristin Erickson, Krysia Bebick, and the honorary "K," Carter Shanklin.

And, thanks to Lucy Guerrero, Alex Polack, and Cliff Sadler of Doc-Express, who were kind enough to help out with some of the diagrams on short notice.

Finally, I'd like to acknowledge Bob Martin, who has continually impressed upon me the need to present OOA&D and UML modeling in simple and straightforward terms, as a source of inspiration for this book.

Doug Rosenberg
Santa Monica, California
February 1999
dougr@iconixsw.com
http://www.iconixsw.com/Doug

Chapter 1

The ICONIX Unified Object Modeling Approach

Figure 1-1 is the "big picture" that shows the key elements of the ICONIX approach. It appears, in various forms, throughout the book.

This book details the ICONIX Unified Object Modeling approach. The approach evolved from my company's practical application of theory presented by the "three amigos"—Grady Booch, Jim Rumbaugh, and

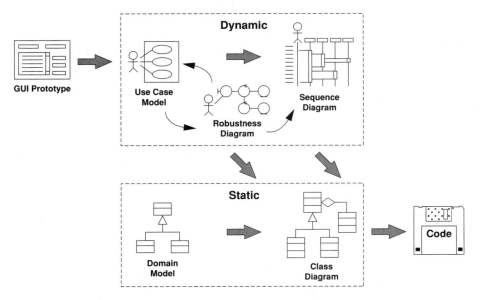

Figure 1-1 *The ICONIX Unified Object Modeling Approach*

1

Ivar Jacobson—in dozens of onsite training workshops that I've conducted over the past several years for companies in a wide variety of industries, starting well before the advent of the UML. I can summarize the essence of the approach in six words: ***driving object models from use cases***.

Healthy portions of this approach are based on Jacobson's Objectory process, defined in *Object-Oriented Software Engineering: A Use Case Driven Approach* (Addison-Wesley, 1992). A key passage defines the phrase **use case driven**:

> When we wish to change the system behavior, we remodel the appropriate actor and use case. The whole system architecture will be controlled by what the users wish to do with the system. As we have traceability through all models, we will be able to modify the system from new requirements. We ask the users what they want to change (which use case) and see directly where these changes should be made in the other models.

The motivation for this book is easy to explain. Benefits of a use case driven approach are so great that they have become obvious to a wide range of people. Yet over the past five years, it has become clear to me that an enormous amount of confusion exists about the practical details of how to drive object models from use cases. This book attempts to resolve that confusion.

The key difference between this book and the amigos' forthcoming book about the Rational Unified Process (RUP) involves "altitude." I see the brilliant methodologists who created the UML as operating at, say, 30,000 feet above the earth, while I'm more like 1,000 feet off the ground, helping people take the great OO ideas and use them every day to build great software systems.

The Rational Unified Process has now superseded Objectory. According to Rational, this process unifies "best practices" involving business modeling, requirements management, component-based development (including support for CORBA and COM), and other areas of software development. Like Objectory and the approach I'm writing about, it's use case driven.

As I write this, the RUP is still very new. I'm sure it will be well received, but there won't be much empirical data available for a while.

There have been other high-visibility attempts to combine major methodologies within one approach or process—for instance, Hewlett-

Packard's Fusion. However, given that customers in more than 40 countries have purchased CD-ROM tutorials about the ICONIX approach, I think it's safe to say that there are few, if any, people whose unified modeling approaches have been introduced to more projects in the field. Visit **http://www.iconixsw.com/CDcourses.html** for more information about these tutorials.

Background

The landscape was littered with object-oriented (OO) methods books between 1991 and 1993. One could just about join the Method of the Month Club. At that time, I was the creator of a multi-method object-oriented analysis and design (OOA&D) visual modeling tool trying to:

- Determine which methods my company should incorporate into the tool (no available method seemed sufficient on its own).
- Teach our clients how to succeed with the various methods we were already supporting.
- Explain to the public why we thought multiple methods made more sense than any single method.

Sitting at this vantage point forced us to evaluate all the viable OO methods that were out there, and to identify the strengths and weaknesses of each. When we did this, some clear synergies between approaches became obvious.

At the beginning of 1993, it became clear to us at ICONIX that there were three major schools of thought emerging in the object-oriented methods community.

We called these schools *data-centered* (derived largely from entity-relationship modeling), *scenario-based*, and *structural* (focused on the structure of the code).

Data-centered methods build on techniques familiar to people who have experience doing structured analysis and design. This category includes Shlaer/Mellor, Martin/Odell, and Rumbaugh's OMT. These methods include the likes of entity-relationship diagrams (ERDs), data-flow diagrams (DFDs), and state-transition diagrams. A data-centered method decomposes a system along data boundaries.

Structural methods start with an OO programming perspective and work from the ground up. The methods developed by Grady Booch and, to a lesser extent, Rebecca Wirfs-Brock (which feature items such as Class-Responsibility-Collaboration [CRC] cards) qualify as structural methods. (As we'll see later, the Wirfs-Brock method is best described as responsibility-driven. We'll learn more about this philosophy during interaction modeling, in Chapter 5.)

Scenario-based methods are grounded in usage scenarios. In addition to Jacobson, the Object Behavior Analysis (OBA) methodology developed by ParcPlace (now ParcPlace-DigitalkObjectShare) and the Alger/Goldstein method are scenario-based. A scenario-based method decomposes a system along usage boundaries.

Around 1993, the "best of breed" within each category seemed to be, respectively, Rumbaugh's Object Modeling Technique (OMT), Jacobson's Object-Oriented Software Engineering (OOSE), and Booch's methodology (usually referred to as the Booch method). We looked hard at the strengths and weaknesses of each and published a series of articles in *OBJECT* magazine, which focused on the best ways to use the three together. The articles include:

- "Using the Object Modeling Technique with Objectory for Client/Server Development" (November 1993)
- "Modeling Client/Server Systems" (March 1994)
- "Validating the Design of Client/Server Systems" (July 1994)
- "Applying O-O Methods to Interactive Multimedia Projects" (June 1995)

I also made two presentations related to this at OOP95 in Munich, in January 1995, "Mixing Rumbaugh OMT with Jacobson Objectory for Client/Server Development" and "An Overview of Object Oriented Analysis and Design Methods." In addition, in 1996, I completed a double CD-ROM, titled *A Unified Object Modeling Approach* (also available through ICONIX), which serves as the foundation for this book.

I can summarize these strengths and weaknesses as follows.

- Booch is very strong in the areas of detailed design and implementation. Analysis receives relatively little attention.
- OMT offers solid tools and techniques for exploring the "problem space" associated with a new system. However, the "solution space" doesn't receive comparable attention. (See Chapter 5 for explanations of these terms.)

- OOSE/Objectory, on the other hand, is extremely useful with regard to the solution space. This method deemphasizes the problem space, though, and there is not enough useful information about how to proceed past the high-level design phase.

In 1993, we synthesized the three approaches into one coherent unified approach. This new approach borrowed most heavily from Jacobson's Objectory process, but it also used OMT for high-level static models and Booch for detailed static and dynamic models.

Our analysis was completely independent and unbiased. We committed this course to CD-ROM while the three amigos were working at different companies and well before the effort that produced the UML got under way. Our Unified approach remains 100 percent valid in the context of the UML.

The biggest problem with having three notations designed by three visionary authors was that it was difficult to convince anyone (unless they had read all three books) that they should follow any kind of unified approach. That these authors have synthesized their work into a unified form that leverages the strengths of each author's original work is unusual, commendable, and very useful. As a result, the UML does an excellent job of providing a single notation that supports the strongest points of each of the three "best of breed" approaches.

Introduction to the Approach

The Unified Booch/Rumbaugh/Jacobson approach that ICONIX has been supporting and teaching since 1993 is based on finding the answers to some fundamentally important questions about a system. These questions include:

1. Who are the users of the system (the actors), and what are they trying to do?
2. What are the "real world" (problem domain) objects and the associations among them?
3. What objects are needed for each use case?
4. How do the objects collaborating within each use case interact?
5. How will we handle real-time control issues?
6. How are we really going to build this system on a nuts-and-bolts level?

I have yet to come across a system that doesn't need to have these basic questions answered, or one that couldn't use the techniques described in this book to help answer them using an iterative, incremental, opportunistic (when you see the answer, capture it) approach. Until recently, one had to piece techniques together from the individual methodologies. What's nice about the UML is that now, the techniques are conveniently collected together in the context of one notation.

Table 1-1 shows which methodology provided us with the best answer to each question, along with the corresponding UML tool or technique.

Although the full approach does present the steps in a specific order, it's not crucial that you follow the steps in that order. Many a project has died a horrible death because of a heavy, restrictive, overly prescriptive "cement collar" process, and I am by no means a proponent of this approach. What I am saying is that *missing answers to any of these questions will add a significant amount of risk to a development effort.*

Let's look again at the top-level view of the ICONIX Unified Object Modeling approach that evolved from our efforts at method synthesis. (See Figure 1-2.)

Table 1-1 *Questions and Answers*

	OOSE	OMT	Booch	UML Tool/Technique
Users and user actions?	•			Use cases
"Real world" objects?		•		High-level (coarsely grained) class diagrams
Objects for each use case?	•			Robustness analysis
Object interactions?	•		•	Sequence and collaboration diagrams
Real-time control issues?	•	•	•	State diagrams
How to build?			•	Low-level (finely grained) class diagrams

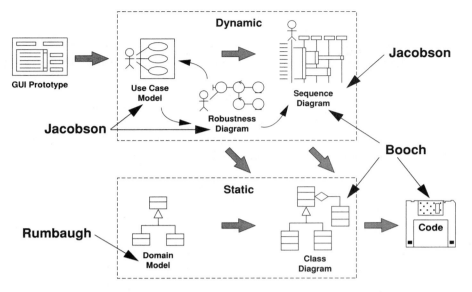

Figure 1-2 *The ICONIX Approach, Showing Three Amigos' Contributions*

As you can see, integrating the best elements of the Booch, Rumbaugh, and Jacobson approaches provides a very complete picture for object-oriented software development.

I'd like to highlight three significant features of this approach.

1. The approach is *iterative* and *incremental*. Multiple iterations occur between developing the domain model and identifying and analyzing the use cases. Other iterations exist, as well, as the team proceeds through the lifecycle. The static model gets refined incrementally during the successive iterations through the dynamic model (composed of use cases, robustness analysis, and sequence diagrams).

2. The approach offers a high degree of *traceability*. At every step along the way, you refer back to the requirements in some way. There is never a point at which the process allows you to stray too far from the user's needs. Traceability also refers to the fact that you can track objects from step to step, as well, as analysis melds into design.

3. The approach offers *streamlined usage of the UML*. The steps I describe in subsequent chapters represent a "minimalist" approach—they

comprise the minimal set of steps that I've found to be necessary and sufficient on the road to a successful OO development project. (See my article "UML Applied: Nine Tips to Incorporating UML into Your Project," in the March 1998 issue of *Software Development* magazine.)

I favor an iterative/incremental and traceable strategy over the approach in which one just writes down the static model without bothering to do the use cases. I discovered a few years ago that I was not immune to the "oops, I forgot about that scenario" error.

In fact, I haven't met many people (or teams) who are immune to the same error. It's a very comforting feeling, for both your team and your prospective users (not to mention your clients), to know that you have actually worked through all the use cases.

In keeping with the last item in the previous list, a recurring theme of this book is **analysis paralysis**—specifically, how to avoid it. I've used the following icon throughout the text in connection with this phenomenon:

Whenever I spot a case of AP coming on, I usually think about Shakespeare's *Much Ado About Nothing*, because the nature of modeling (and of "kitchen sink" notations such as the UML) makes it easy to generate lots of "sound and fury, signifying nothing." You'll find that, wherever possible, I advocate "less is more."

The ICONIX approach has helped produce systems for video on demand, healthcare claims processing, retail point of sale, aerospace launch control, retail purchase order management, financial portfolio management, command and control systems, and vehicle navigation, among others. The rest of this book provides details that I hope will enable you to use the approach to build great systems.

Thoughts on Methodology

In developing the ICONIX Unified approach, we had to violate, to some extent, the rules and semantics of all three approaches that served as the primary building blocks. This was undoubtedly considered a heretic act by some true believers of the individual methodologies, although not by their creators. (See the appendix for more encounters with true believers.) I would do it again without hesitation, however, and I will continue to refine my approach as the three amigos refine and expand the UML.

This book does *not* suggest that you should abandon all guidelines and rules of methodology. However, projects run into problems when methodology becomes dogma.

Tom DeMarco calls this "capital-M methodology," which we might represent as **M**ethodology (as opposed to methodology). DeMarco subsequently indicated that one of his key indicators of a successful project occurs when the project team tailors the methodology to the individual needs of the project rather than attempt to force-fit the project into the **M**ethodology. DeMarco calls this a sign of "a project with its brain switched to the ON position."

The point is that no matter how brilliant and experienced a methodologist is, there are always some situations that are less than perfect fits for a particular approach. When methodology becomes religion (**M**ethodology) and is followed by rote rather than being followed because it leads to the desired result, major problems occur and projects fail. Software can't be developed on autopilot—it requires thought.

My suggestion is simply this: Use methodology to guide your modeling effort. Follow it as closely as possible within reason. If you find yourself getting all twisted up trying to satisfy some fairly minor restriction of the methodology, don't be afraid to switch on your brain and adapt the methodology to your problem. And if you come across a potentially useful technique, do your best to bend the methodology to accommodate it. (Plus, as far as I know, no one is offering awards for most rigorous compliance with the UML *Semantics* document.)

Process Fundamentals

I believe the best way to make process more attractive is to educate as many people as possible about the benefits of answering the questions I raised earlier, along with similar questions, and to the risks of failing to answer them. It is straightforward to build good object models *if you keep ruthlessly focused on answering the fundamentally important questions about the system you are building and refuse to get caught up in superfluous modeling issues*. That philosophy lies at the heart of the ICONIX Unified Object Modeling approach.

The people who have to use the process, and management, are both customers of a software development process. I think of a process as a road map for a team to follow, a map that identifies a set of landmarks, or *milestones*, along the way to producing a quality product.

There are various paths a team can travel, depending on the capabilities and preferences of its members. But no matter which path they go down, at some point, they must reach the milestones. It is at these points in the process that their work becomes visible to management—during reviews of intermediate results. Passing the milestones does not guarantee a quality product, but it should greatly improve the chances.

I believe milestones for an object-oriented process should include, at a minimum, the following.

• The team has identified and described all the usage scenarios for the system it's about to build.

• The team has taken a hard look for reusable abstractions (classes) that participate in multiple scenarios.

• The team has thought about the problem domain and has identified classes that belong to that domain—in other words, the team has thought about reusability beyond just this system.

• The team has verified that all functional requirements of the system are accounted for in the design.

• The team has thought carefully about how the required system behavior gets allocated to the identified abstractions, taking into consideration good design principles such as minimizing coupling, maximizing cohesion, generality, sufficiency, and so forth.

Beyond these milestones, there are at least four other fundamental requirements of a process.

1. It has to be flexible enough to accommodate different styles and kinds of problems.

2. It has to support the way people really work (including prototyping and iterative/incremental development).

3. It needs to serve as a guide for less-experienced members of the team, helping them be as productive as possible without handcuffing more-experienced members.

4. It needs to expose the pre-code products of a development effort to management in a reasonably standard and comprehensible form.

The Approach in a Nutshell

The basic steps that comprise the full ICONIX Unified Object Modeling approach and the associated milestones are presented in Figure 1-3 through Figure 1-6. Note that these diagrams will appear again later in the text to remind you where we are in the overall approach.

• Identify your real-world domain objects and the generalization and aggregation relationships among those objects. Start drawing a high-level class diagram.

• If it's feasible, do some rapid prototyping of the proposed system. Or gather whatever substantive information you have about the legacy system you are reengineering.

• Identify your use cases, using use case diagrams.

• Organize the use cases into groups. Capture this organization in a package diagram.

• Allocate functional requirements to the use cases and domain objects at this stage.

Milestone 1: Requirements Review

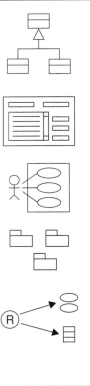

Figure 1-3 *Requirements Analysis*

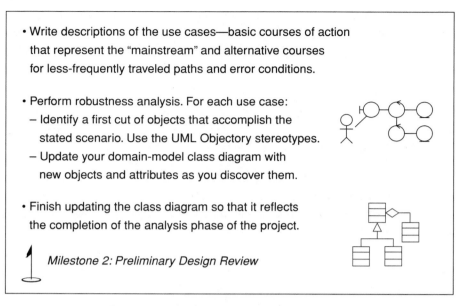

- Write descriptions of the use cases—basic courses of action
  that represent the "mainstream" and alternative courses
  for less-frequently traveled paths and error conditions.

- Perform robustness analysis. For each use case:
  – Identify a first cut of objects that accomplish the
    stated scenario. Use the UML Objectory stereotypes.
  – Update your domain-model class diagram with
    new objects and attributes as you discover them.

- Finish updating the class diagram so that it reflects
  the completion of the analysis phase of the project.

  Milestone 2: Preliminary Design Review

Figure 1-4 *Analysis and Preliminary Design*

These diagrams together illustrate three key principles that underlie the approach, which, as you can see, is inside-out, outside-in, and top-down, all at the same time.

1. Work inward from the user requirements.

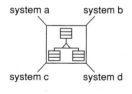

2. Work outward from the data requirements.

3. Drill down from high-level models to detailed design.

I'll reinforce these principles, in one way or another, in each subsequent chapter. I suggest that if you adopt them at the beginning of a software development project and stick with them, you will significantly increase your chances of success.

• Allocate behavior. For each use case:
  – Identify the messages that need to be passed between objects,
    the objects, and the associated methods to be invoked.
    Draw a sequence diagram with use case text running
    down the left side and design information on the right.
    Continue to update the class diagram with attributes
    and operations as you find them.
  – If you wish, use a collaboration diagram to show
    the key transactions between objects.
  – If you wish, use a state diagram to show the real-time behavior.

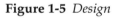

• Finish the static model by adding detailed design
  information (for instance, visibility values and patterns).

• Verify with your team that your design satisfies
  all the requirements you've identified.

Milestone 3: Detailed/Critical Design Review

Figure 1-5 *Design*

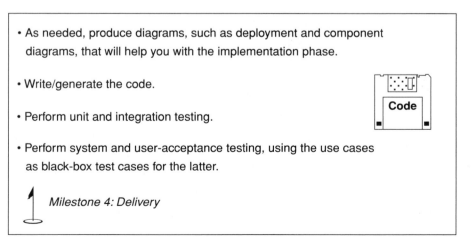

• As needed, produce diagrams, such as deployment and component
  diagrams, that will help you with the implementation phase.

• Write/generate the code.

• Perform unit and integration testing.

• Perform system and user-acceptance testing, using the use cases
  as black-box test cases for the latter.

Milestone 4: Delivery

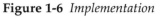

Figure 1-6 *Implementation*

Chapter 2

Domain Modeling

The term **problem domain** refers to the area that encompasses real-world things and concepts related to the problem that the system is being designed to solve. **Domain modeling** is the task of discovering "objects" (classes, actually) that represent those things and concepts.

Within the ICONIX Unified Object Modeling approach, domain modeling involves working outward from the data requirements to build a *static* model of the problem domain relevant to the proposed system, as shown in Figure 2-1.

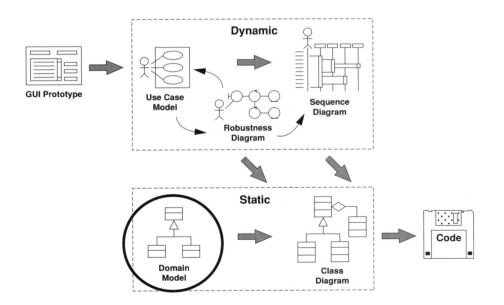

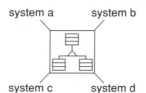

Figure 2-1 *Working Outward from Data Requirements*

This "inside-out" approach contrasts with the "outside-in" approach we take toward user requirements, as I describe in Chapter 3. This enables us to perform these efforts in parallel, as shown in the diagram at the beginning of the chapter.

Chapter 4 describes how the domain modeling and use case development paths merge. In combination with later chapters, the text in Chapter 4 reinforces the principle, central to the approach, that *the dynamic model drives the static model*. The domain model thus serves as a *glossary of terms* that writers of use cases can use in the early stages of that effort. (This is the main reason why I talk about domain modeling before use cases.)

Please note that I am *not* interested in adding more fuel to the static-modeling fire. Plenty of books are devoted to this subject, and this book isn't intended to be one more.

Rather, the goal of this chapter is to emphasize domain modeling more than Jacobson's original process did. When my colleagues and I formulated our Unified approach, it was clear that Jacobson's treatment of domain modeling was relatively weak compared with that of OMT, so we borrowed from Rumbaugh.

I like to "jump start" domain modeling by making a quick pass through the available relevant material, highlighting nouns as I go while also making at least mental notes about verbs and possessive phrases for future reference. (See Kurt Derr's *Applying OMT* [SIGS Books, 1995] for more information about this "grammatical inspection" technique.) I've found that after refining the lists as work progresses:

- *Nouns* and *noun phrases* become **objects** and **attributes.**
- *Verbs* and *verb phrases* become **operations** and **associations.**
- *Possessive phrases* indicate that nouns should be **attributes** rather than **objects.**

I refer to these concepts in several sections that describe the key activities that comprise domain modeling within the ICONIX approach.

Discover Classes

Jim Rumbaugh defines a **class** as "a description of a group of objects with similar properties, common behavior, common relationships, and common semantics." The first thing you need to do in building a static model of your system is to find appropriate classes that accurately represent the real abstractions the problem domain presents. If you execute this activity well, you will have not only a solid foundation on which to build the system, but also excellent prospects for *reuse* by systems that will be designed and built down the line. (Other systems that you build can share these domain classes.)

The best sources of classes are likely to be:

*   The high-level problem statement
*   Lower-level requirements
*   Expert knowledge of the problem space

To get started on the road to discovery, lay out as many relevant statements from these areas (and even others such as marketing literature) as you can find, and then circle, or highlight, all the nouns and noun phrases. Chances are good that you will find a large majority of the important domain objects (classes) this way.

Figure 2-2 contains a set of requirements from an example system, which we'll call Portfolio Trading and Accounting, with the nouns and noun phrases in bold.

Figure 2-3 shows what we have after we eliminate the duplicate terms, make plural terms singular, and put the results in alphabetical order.

The next step is to sift through your list of candidate classes and eliminate the items that are unnecessary (because they're redundant or irrelevant) or incorrect (because they're too vague, or they represent things or concepts outside the scope of the model, or they represent actions even though they're phrased as nouns).

The **Portfolio Manager** shall be able to roll up **portfolios** on several **levels**.

A **Trader** shall be able to place **orders**, on behalf of a **portfolio**, that generate one or more trades.

A **Portfolio Manager** shall be able to select a **pairoff method** in conjunction with placing a **sell order**.

The **entry** of a **trade** shall generate **forecasted cashflows** associated with the given **trade lot**.

The **system** shall match up **actual cashflows** with **forecasted cashflows**.

The **system** shall automatically generate appropriate **postings** to the **General Ledger**.

The **system** shall allow an **Assistant Trader** to modify **trade data** and propagate the **results** appropriately.

Figure 2-2 *Nouns in Example System Requirements*

Here's how the thought process might go with regard to our list.

1. *Assistant Trader, Portfolio Manager,* and *Trader* are actors, and thus should be placed on use case diagrams.
2. The word *entry* implies action, so it's not a class. (It may turn out later to be an operation.)

actual cashflow	order	sell order
Assistant Trader	pairoff method	system
entry	portfolio	trade
forecasted cashflow	Portfolio Manager	trade data
General Ledger	posting	trade lot
level	results	Trader

Figure 2-3 *First Set of Candidate Classes for Example System*

3. *General Ledger* is an entity that lies outside the scope of the project; the users have yet to define much in the way of accounting features they want to see. Because we have *posting* already, which we know will be within the scope, let's take *General Ledger* out of our list.

4. Looking at the first requirement again, we see that the word *level* is closely tied to the verb phrase *roll portfolios up*, so we should make a note and set *level* aside for now.

5. The word *results* and the phrase *trade data* are too vague to be of particular use.

6. We have both *order* and *sell order*. Because we don't know much about the nature of an *order* yet, except that given the presence of a sell order, there's probably a need for a buy order, as well, let's focus on *order* for now and address "buy" and "sell" later. Note, though, that buy and sell are "kinds of" orders.

7. The word *system* is too vague to be the name of an object.

The results appear in Figure 2-4, with proper class names.

Just as the initial list looked rather too large, this list appears to be a little thin. At this point, we need to go back and discover more classes by reading between the lines of the problem statement and requirements, and by exploring the available domain expertise further. Within our example system, we uncover six more classes by writing out the following statements.

*   A trade involves a particular *Investment*.
*   A portfolio holds *Position*s in a number of investments.
*   The primary data entered for a trade needs to be persistent, so we need a *TradeAdjustment* class that will hold modified data for trades.
*   The system also needs a way to keep information about *DisposedTradeLot*s associated with *Sell Order*s.

ActualCashflow	PairoffMethod	Sell Order
Buy Order	Portfolio	Trade
ForecastedCashflow	Posting	TradeLot

Figure 2-4 *Refined Set of Candidate Classes*

- We forgot to address the pairing of actual and forecasted cash-flows, so we need a class for that. We'll call it *TradeLotActualCashflow*, because a forecasted cashflow is always tied to a trade lot. (This is a "link" class, which we'll discuss later in the chapter.)
- A posting involves a particular account, and we do have some idea about how things should work at the account level, so we need a *GLAccount* class (where *GL* is an abbreviation of General Ledger).

Before we continue with the example system, please note that although I find grammatical inspection techniques useful in getting a quick start on the domain model, I do *not* advocate spending months, weeks, or even days using such techniques. (As we'll see in Chapter 4, we discovered the rest of the objects for our system during robustness analysis.)

 It's important to place limits on the time you spend on this kind of analysis; otherwise, analysis paralysis will likely rear its ugly head. I usually find that a couple of hours is enough time to find the majority of important objects in a situation, and I would hesitate to exceed a half-day of noun/verb analysis.

ALERT! *Don't get bogged down in grammatical inspection.*

There are other refinements to be made, but we'll defer those to the next couple of sections, where they will highlight a major element of the approach: *continuous improvement via ongoing iteration and refinement.* In the meantime, Figure 2-5 contains our current list of classes.

Figure 2-6 illustrates two notations you can use to represent a class on a class diagram. The one on the left shows the full form. Because we're

ActualCashflow	*Investment*	*Sell Order*
Buy Order	*PairoffMethod*	*Trade*
DisposedTradeLot	*Portfolio*	*TradeAdjustment*
ForecastedCashflow	*Position*	*TradeLot*
GLAccount	*Posting*	*TradeLotActualCashflow*

Figure 2-5 *Candidate Classes After Further Refinement*

Figure 2-6 *Class Notations*

trying to show the "big picture" of our domain model for now, however, I also provide a more compact notation, on the right, which you can use before you know the other elements of a given class. I use this simpler notation in the rest of this chapter, for the most part, and then switch to full class boxes throughout the rest of the book.

Build Generalization Relationships

A **generalization** is a relationship in which one class is a refinement of another class. Another term for a generalization is **kind-of relationship**, where one class is a kind of another class. Some people like to use the phrase "is-a" in describing this.) Within this relationship, the former class is called the **superclass**, or **parent**, while the latter class is the **subclass**, or **child**.

The subclass inherits the attributes and methods defined for the superclass, and also the associations in which the superclass is involved. The subclass can use these features of its superclass as is, or it can modify them for more-specialized purposes. You can also add attributes and methods to the subclass that aren't available to the superclass.

Within our example system, *Trade* and *Investment* are good candidates for subtyping.

In the first section of this chapter, "Discover Classes," I indicated that because we don't know much about the nature of an *order* yet, we should focus on *order* and look at *sell order* later. This is the right time to take another look.

As we've delved more deeply into the user's needs for the new system, we've discovered that there are indeed aspects of buy and sell orders that are different enough to justify separate treatment, while they still have enough in common that both are kinds of *Order*.

However, we know that an *Order* generates a *Trade*. It's also the case that the differences between buying and selling seem to relate more to the nature of a *Trade* than to that of an *Order*. So let's attach the concepts of buy and sell to *Trade* and focus on how *Trade* lends itself to generalizations.

Two new classes, named *Buy* and *Sell*, inherit the attributes and methods we've defined for *Trade*. We'll add one new attribute called assumedPrice to *Buy*. And we'll note that *Buy* will now be the class that sends "create" messages to *TradeLot*, and *Sell* will send messages to *TradeLot* about that class's disposeQuantity method.

Sell also needs a method named disposeTradeLots, because a *Trade* might dispose of more than one *TradeLot*.

Note that we've discovered these attributes and operations "ahead of schedule." We'll discuss identifying attributes in Chapter 4 and assigning operations to classes in Chapter 5.

Figure 2-7 shows the notation for this generalization structure.

If you need to, and you're comfortable doing so at this stage of the process, you can generalize to more than one level of subclass. Remember to look for kind-of statements that are true in the "real world."

Figure 2-8 shows the results of a preliminary analysis of the *Investment* class within our example system.

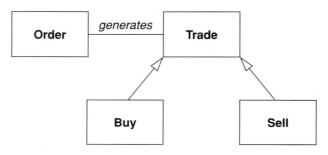

Figure 2-7 *Generalization of Trade Class*

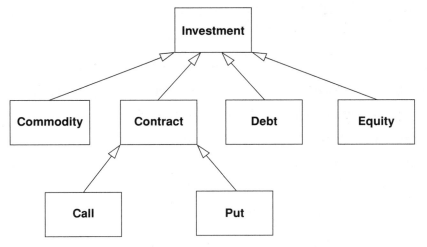

Figure 2-8 *Generalization of Investment Class*

Build Associations Between Classes

An **association** is a static relationship between two classes. Associations show dependencies between classes, but *not* actions (even though they are verb phrases). Actions involving two classes are best captured by operations and messages, as I describe in Chapter 5.

Much like an entity-relationship diagram (ERD), our domain model, updated to show associations, should be a ***true statement about the problem space, independent of time*** (that is, ***static***). This model serves as the foundation of our static class model.

Build your list of candidate associations from your list of verbs and verb phrases and also from your knowledge of the problem domain, requirements, and so forth. Refine the list by removing anything that clearly states an action rather than a dependency or that's specifically related to implementation or is otherwise not relevant during this phase of the process.

Figure 2-9 contains a first cut at a list of associations for the currently known classes within our example system.

ActualCashflow **matches up with** *TradeLotActualCashflow*	*Posting* **relates to** *TradeLot*
Order **generates** *Trades*	*Trade* **generates** *DisposedTradeLots*
Portfolio **places** *Orders*	*Trade* **generates** *ForecastedCashflows*
Portfolio **has** *PairoffMethod*	*Trade* **involves** *Investment*
Portfolio **holds** *Position*	*Trade* **generates** *TradeLot*
Position **is in** *Investment*	*TradeAdjustment* **corresponds with** *Trade*
Posting **involves** *GLAccount*	*TradeLot* **has** *ForecastedCashflows*
TradeLot **matches up with** *TradeLotActualCashflows*	

Figure 2-9 *Candidate Associations*

Note that some of these associations represent one-to-one relation-ships while others represent one-to-many relationships. In the UML, one-to-one and one-to-many are referred to as **multiplicities**.

 You don't need to worry at this stage about being more spe-cific about the numbers on the many side of one-to-many associations. These are details you will address later in the project. Actually, you can avoid dealing with multiplicity altogether during domain modeling—it chews up time and can be a major cause of analysis paralysis.

ALERT! *Don't address multiplicity too early in the project.*

Figure 2-10 shows how associations appear on class diagrams.

Figure 2-10 *Association Notation*

I recommend that wherever possible, you place your associations so that they read left to right and top to bottom, just as you would regular text. This will improve the readability of your diagrams.

You can see that some verbs in the associations in our example system (for instance, *generates*) are action verbs. We'll look at these more closely during sequence diagramming, in Chapter 5. Meanwhile, we can make further refinements involving two special types of associations.

An **aggregation** is an association in which one class is made up of other classes. I like to refer to aggregations as "piece-part" relationships, in which the component classes are smaller pieces or parts of the larger whole class. Just as the term *kind-of relationship* described generalization, we can define an aggregation as a **part-of relationship**. (Some folks prefer to use "has" instead of "part of." In fact, Booch originally described "has by reference" and "has by value" relationships.)

The UML also offers a construct named **composition**, which is a strong form of aggregation in which a "piece" class is "owned by" one larger class. Composition evolved from the Booch "has by value" relationship.

 I'm not going to address composition here, because after reading several hundred postings on the Object Technology User Group (OTUG), run by Rational, about aggregation versus composition, it occurs to me that when this kind of tail-chasing occurs too early in a software development project, static modeling—in the absence of a proper use case model—is often a dead end. I much prefer to focus on simple aggregation during domain modeling. Aggregation versus composition is a detailed design issue.

ALERT! *Don't worry about aggregation and composition until detailed design.*

Within the example, we made a note about rolling up portfolios. Specifically, this is the requirement: "The Portfolio Manager shall be able to roll up portfolios on several levels." We can address this requirement now by way of an aggregation. This requires creating a new class, which we might as well call *PortfolioRollup*. We also need two new associations.

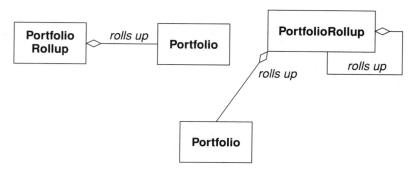

Figure 2-11 *Aggregation*

1. *PortfolioRollup* **contains** *Portfolios*
2. *PortfolioRollup* **contains** *PortfolioRollups*

So the new *PortfolioRollup* class contains two kinds of aggregation: regular aggregation and what we might refer to as self-aggregation. Figure 2-11 shows how we represent both of them.

Develop Association Classes

Looking more closely at our list of associations, we notice there are two classes that serve as "pairing" mechanisms: *Position* pairs *Investment* and *Portfolio*; *TradeLotActualCashflow* pairs *ActualCashflow* and *TradeLot*. These pairing classes are called **association classes,** or **link classes,** because they serve to link classes, as do associations, but they also have properties that are independent of those classes.

Association classes often arise in situations in which there are many-to-many multiplicities within the data model. This is one subject that OMT handled better than other data-centered methods.

Most domain models I've seen over the years have at least one or two link classes. However, you need to be careful not to overuse this construct.

Figure 2-12 illustrates how we would draw this special association.

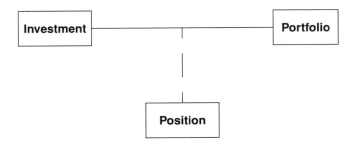

Figure 2-12 *Association Class*

Mine Your Legacy Documentation for Domain Classes

If you're reengineering a legacy system that uses a relational database (RDB), the tables within that database are likely to be another excellent source of domain classes. However, you have to be careful not to just bring them over to your static model wholesale. Relational tables can have lots of attributes that might not belong together in the context of an object model.

Figure 2-13 shows a class that would make it into our sample system's static model if we were to bring it over intact from the associated RDB table in the original system.

As you can see, this class is enormous. However, by rearranging the attributes the way we have, it's easy to spot logical groupings. For instance, Acctg Appr Code and Post Date are both related to accounting, and there is a set of six attributes associated with trade settlement and closing.

We can use aggregation to factor these attribute groups into what I refer to as **helper classes**. These are classes that contain attributes and operations that are relevant to more-significant classes. (This illustrates a fundamental difference between an OO approach and an approach that relies on relational database management systems [RDBMSs]: we don't want a class called *Kitchen Sink*!)

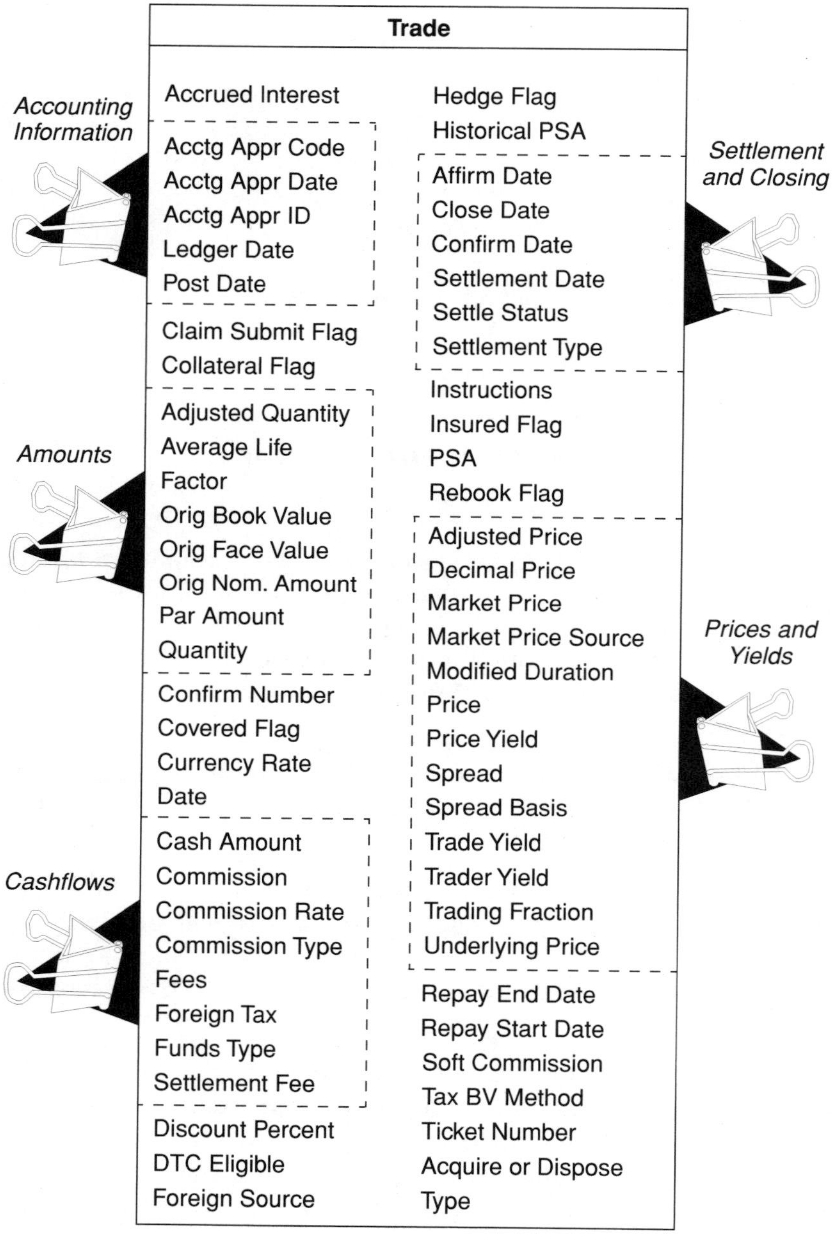

Trade

Accounting Information

Accrued Interest

Acctg Appr Code
Acctg Appr Date
Acctg Appr ID
Ledger Date
Post Date

Claim Submit Flag
Collateral Flag

Amounts

Adjusted Quantity
Average Life
Factor
Orig Book Value
Orig Face Value
Orig Nom. Amount
Par Amount
Quantity

Confirm Number
Covered Flag
Currency Rate
Date

Cashflows

Cash Amount
Commission
Commission Rate
Commission Type
Fees
Foreign Tax
Funds Type
Settlement Fee

Discount Percent
DTC Eligible
Foreign Source

Hedge Flag
Historical PSA

Affirm Date
Close Date
Confirm Date
Settlement Date
Settle Status
Settlement Type

Settlement and Closing

Instructions
Insured Flag
PSA
Rebook Flag

Adjusted Price
Decimal Price
Market Price
Market Price Source
Modified Duration
Price
Price Yield
Spread
Spread Basis
Trade Yield
Trader Yield
Trading Fraction
Underlying Price

Prices and Yields

Repay End Date
Repay Start Date
Soft Commission
Tax BV Method
Ticket Number
Acquire or Dispose
Type

Figure 2-13 *Oversize Trade Class, Ripe for Factoring*

Figure 2-14 shows the helper classes we created for *Trade* based on these attribute groupings, along with helpers for other big classes.

Figure 2-15 shows the original contents of what will become our *Investment* class. Figure 2-16 shows the associated helper classes.

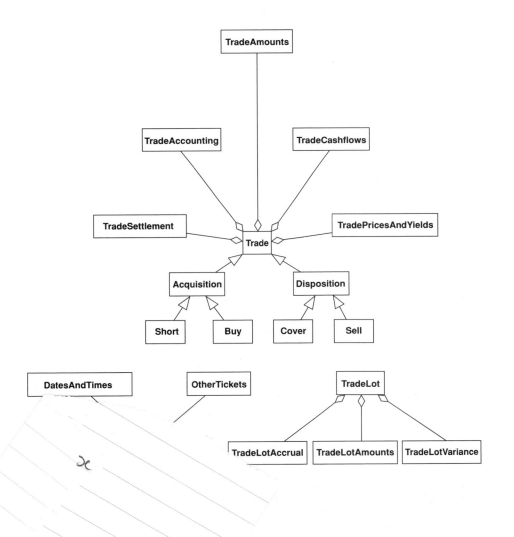

Helper Classes (Part 1)

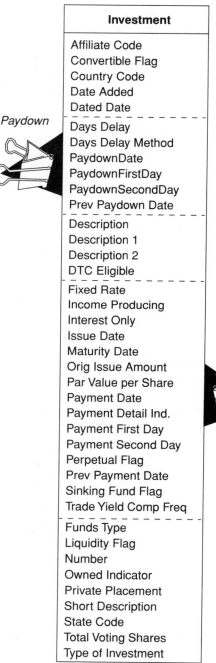

Paydown

Payment

Figure 2-15 *Oversize Investment Class, Ripe for Factoring*

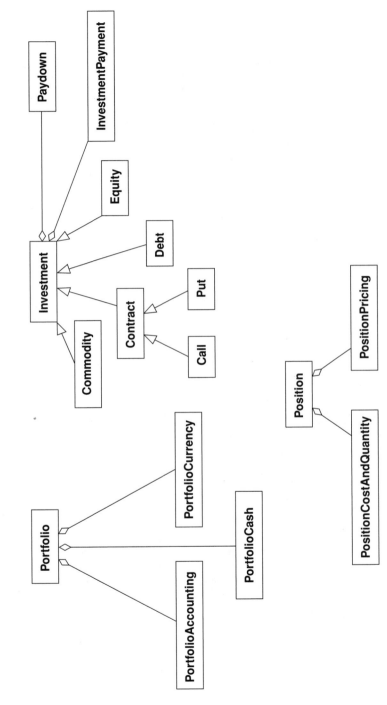

Figure 2-16 *Helper Classes (Part 2)*

Draw an Analysis-Level Class Diagram

I've described each of the elements that comprise a class diagram at the analysis level. I've also shown the various notations you use to capture these elements. When you are reasonably satisfied with the results of the previous tasks—discovering classes, building associations, generalizing—it's time to put the pieces together on one diagram.

Figure 2-14 and Figure 2-16 show chunks of the full static model at this stage of our example system project. Figure 2-17 shows the rest of this model—the relationships among all the main classes we've identified to date.

Your diagram, like these class diagrams, should include whatever you've decided on to this point, even if that means the diagram

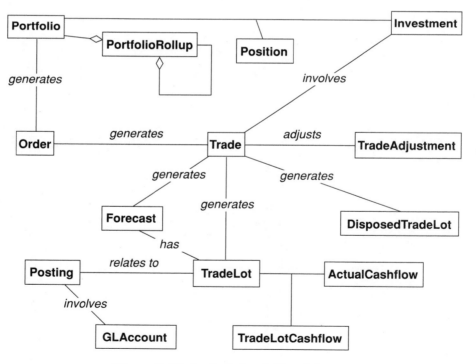

Figure 2-17 *Analysis-Level Class Diagram*

extends over a number of sheets of paper. Your analysis-level class diagram will serve as the foundation for expanded class diagrams at the design and implementation levels later in the process.

Continue to Iterate and Refine

I keep repeating the phrase *iterate and refine*, or variations of it, because I don't want you to lose sight of the fact that the user's needs and wants are the reasons your project team exists. It's also well established that the more time you spend analyzing up front, the less time you're likely to spend tinkering with the system after it's "finished."

However, this does *not* mean that you should keep grinding nouns and verbs (which, in my experience, can happen without warning if you follow Derr's approach [see page 17] too vigilantly) until you turn perfectly good steak into hamburger (and half your team quits as a result), nor should you threaten your analysts with burnout. The goal is to **build a glossary of class names that will serve as the nouns, as appropriate, within your use case text**.

I also recommend that you establish a time budget for building your initial domain model. You should be vigilant about making necessary adjustments to your analysis-level class model in response to occurrences during robustness analysis and throughout the project.

Please note that the diagram you draw during domain modeling, however detailed, is still just a *skeleton* of your object model. Now it's time to add meat to those bones and develop the dynamic model by generating use cases, discussed in Chapter 3; refining the static and dynamic models with robustness analysis, discussed in Chapter 4; and entering detailed design based on the dynamic model with interaction modeling, the subject of Chapter 5. If you're smart, you'll update your static model as you go.

Figure 2-18 shows where we are and where we're headed.

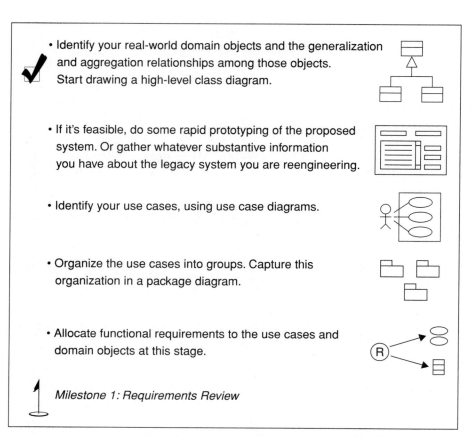

- Identify your real-world domain objects and the generalization and aggregation relationships among those objects. Start drawing a high-level class diagram.

- If it's feasible, do some rapid prototyping of the proposed system. Or gather whatever substantive information you have about the legacy system you are reengineering.

- Identify your use cases, using use case diagrams.

- Organize the use cases into groups. Capture this organization in a package diagram.

- Allocate functional requirements to the use cases and domain objects at this stage.

Milestone 1: Requirements Review

Figure 2-18 *Requirements Analysis Checkpoint 1*

Top 10 Domain Modeling Errors

10. *Start assigning multiplicities to associations right off the bat. Make sure that every association has an explicit multiplicity.*

9. *Do noun and verb analysis so exhaustive that you pass out along the way.*

8. *Assign operations to classes without exploring use cases and sequence diagrams.*

7. *Optimize your code for reusability before making sure you've satisfied the users' requirements.*

6. *Debate whether to use aggregation or composition for each of your part-of associations.*

5. *Presume a specific implementation strategy without modeling the problem space.*

4. *Use hard-to-understand names for your classes—like cPortMgrIntf— instead of intuitively obvious ones, such as PortfolioManager.*

3. *Jump directly to implementation constructs such as friend relationships and parameterized classes.*

2. *Create a one-for-one mapping between domain classes and relational database tables.*

1. *Perform "premature patternization," which involves building cool solutions, from patterns, that have little or no connection to user problems.*

Chapter 3

Use Case Modeling

Within the Unified Object Modeling approach, one of the early steps involves building a **use case model**. The essence of this model is to capture user requirements of a new system, whether it's being developed from scratch or based on an existing system, by detailing all the scenarios that users will be performing.

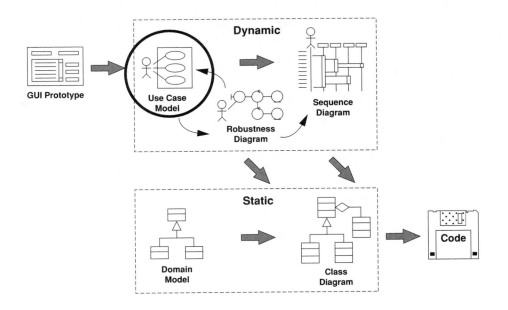

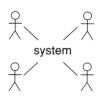

Figure 3-1 *Working Inward from User Requirements*

The use case model is at the conceptual center of the approach because it drives everything that follows, as you can see in the following list of the other key elements of the approach.

- The use case model is developed in cooperation with the domain model (Chapter 2).
- Robustness analysis (Chapter 4) involves identifying a first-cut set of collaborating objects that satisfy each use case.
- Interaction modeling (Chapter 5) is a refinement of the results of robustness analysis that lays out how messages flow between objects within use cases.
- Collaboration and state modeling (Chapter 6) involve exploring the dynamic behavior of objects within use cases.
- Requirements tracing (Chapter 7) involves connecting user requirements with use cases and classes.
- Use cases form the basis for user acceptance tests during the implementation phase (Chapter 8).

The *dynamic* model gets started with use case analysis. This effort involves working inward from the user requirements, as shown in Figure 3-1.

As you'll see from this point forward, use cases do more than get the dynamic model started—rather, they *drive* the dynamic model and, by extension, the entire development effort.

Use Cases, Actors, and Use Case Diagrams

A **use case** is a sequence of actions that an actor (usually a person, but perhaps an external entity, such as another system) performs within a system to achieve a particular goal.

A use case is most effectively stated from the perspective of the user as *a present-tense verb phrase in active voice*. For instance, one use case within a hospital system might be called Admit Patient, while a port-folio system is likely to contain use cases named Do Trade Entry, Update Portfolio Information, and Generate Reports.

A complete and unambiguous use case describes one aspect of usage of the system *without presuming any specific design or implementation*. (How-ever, it is a good idea to name those problem domain objects affected by the user's actions.) The result of use case modeling should be that *all* required system functionality is described in the use cases. If you don't adhere to this basic principle, you run the risk of having your bright engi-neers build a cool system that isn't what your customers want.

An **actor** represents a role a user can play with regard to a system or an entity, such as another system or a database, that will reside outside the system being modeled. The total set of actors within a use case model reflects everything that needs to exchange information with the system. Within a hospital system, actors include *Doctors* and *Administrative Staff*; a portfolio system has actors called *Risk Manager* and *Trader*.

A user can serve as more than one type of actor. For instance, a *Nurse* might perform administrative duties. Similarly, more than one user can appear as a particular actor (for instance, multiple *Trading Assis-tants* interacting with a portfolio system).

We show use cases and actors on a **use case diagram**. Within a use case diagram, use cases appear as ovals, generally in the middle of the dia-gram; actors appear as stick figures to the left and right.

Figure 3-2 is an example of a use case diagram.

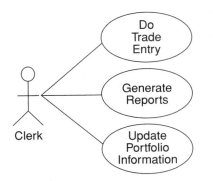

Figure 3-2 *Use Case Diagram*

Analysis-Level and Design-Level Use Cases

A key goal of use case driven object modeling involves identifying objects that can be reused throughout the system. Toward this end, the modeler can generate two types of use cases whose relationship parallels that of a class and an object belonging to that class.

An **analysis-level** (or **business process**) use case represents behavior that is common to a number of use cases. The term *analysis-level* has parallels with the term *abstract* in the context of C++, in that an analysis-level use case is never instantiated. In other words, it will not be used to directly drive an object model. (See Jacobson's *The Object Advantage: Business Process Reengineering with Object Technology* [Addison-Wesley, 1995] for more information.)

A use case that is instantiated is called a **design-level**, or **concrete**, use case. Design-level use cases sometimes use, or at least refer to, part or all of the description of the associated analysis-level use cases.

Take a typical word-processing program. It will have a menu bar option named Format. When the user selects that item, a window appears that offers a variety of choices that we can express in use case terms such as Format Font, Format Paragraph, and Adjust Tabs. Format represents the analysis-level use case; the three options are the design-level use cases. (You might also have a *package* of use cases, named Format, in this situation. I talk about use case packages later in the chapter.)

Writing Use Cases

Now that I've defined some basic terms and concepts, let's talk about how to write use cases.

We'll focus our efforts on design-level use cases, which some people call *scenarios*. You should be able to write a solid paragraph or two about a design-level use case. If you find yourself able to capture the essence of a proposed use case in, say, one sentence, it's likely you're breaking your system usage down too finely.

Just as the development process I describe in this book is an iterative and incremental process, the task of building use cases for your new system is based on identifying as many as you can up front, and then establishing a continuous loop of writing and refining the text that describes them. Along the way, you will discover new use cases, and also factor out commonality in usage.

Working Inward from a GUI to Identify Use Cases

You should keep one overriding principle in mind at all times in your effort to identify use cases: *They should have strong correlations with material in the user manual for the system*. It should be obvious what the connection is between each use case and a distinct section of your user guide. This reinforces the fundamental notion that you are conforming the design of your system to the viewpoints of the users. It also provides a convenient summary of what "use case driven" means: *Write the user manual, then write the code*.

I encourage my clients to use rapid prototyping as frequently as possible. The idea is that developers and users sit down together and build something that will demonstrate "proof of concept."

I've found over the years that the best way to identify chunks of use cases in connection with a prototype is to write a rough user manual, as if the prototype were an actual fully working system. The manual certainly doesn't have to be polished; the idea is to describe the primary functions that users of the "system" perform, in language that's clear and unambiguous.

You will retrieve mostly basic courses of action from a prototype user guide, because by definition, "rapid" prototyping generally involves ignoring alternative courses (that is, exceptions). Be careful about this, though. After all, if all you had to build was a system that addressed basic courses, you'd probably finish ahead of schedule! (I'll reinforce this idea to a healthy extent later in the chapter.)

Taking this idea one step further, I've found that exploring the graphical user interface (GUI) design in parallel with the required system behavior is generally an excellent approach. This involves iterating, with the users, the presentation aspects of the system, and after achieving closure on a couple of screens, writing the associated use cases. This bouncing back and forth can be very effective in the right environment.

If prototyping isn't feasible or desirable in your situation, feel free to write science fiction. I mean that you should put *something* on paper—screen mockups, pseudo-text, whatever—that will help you and your users understand each other and reach at least tentative agreement. It's not that important how close this something is to reality just yet.

If you're worried that prototyping might degenerate into extended GUI design, use line drawings like the one in Figure 3-3. This gives everyone a chance to focus on operational concepts, without getting into the hair-splitting that often occurs when people look at GUI designs. (The arrow to the right of the *Investment* field indicates the need for a drop-down menu.)

Here's how the associated use case might read:

> The trading clerk specifies the trade type. Then the clerk selects the investment involved in that trade from the list of available investments. The clerk also enters the ticket number that appears on the paper ticket for the order. Once all the necessary data is in place, the clerk presses a button to move to the next task.

Notice that the use case doesn't refer to the types of elements that appear in the mockup. The "radio buttons" could very well turn into a drop-down menu tomorrow. But because we've insulated the use case text from the details of the GUI, we've kept the spotlight on what the user needs to do with the system.

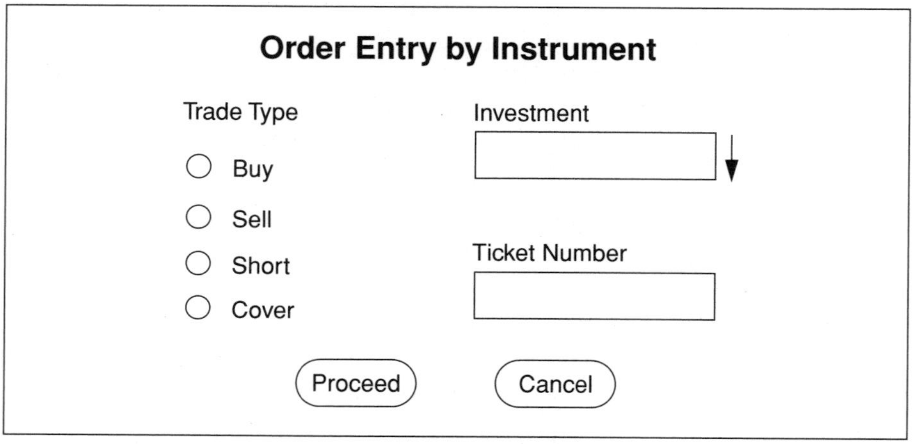

Figure 3-3 *Sample Screen Mockup*

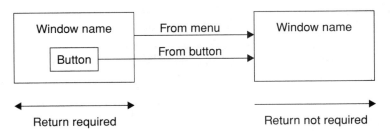

Figure 3-4 *Windows Navigation Diagram Elements*

Another useful approach to "GUI design without the GUI" comes from Meilir Page-Jones, author of the forthcoming book *Fundamentals of Object-Oriented Design in UML*. At the center of his approach is the **windows navigation diagram**, which he and his colleagues at Wayland Systems use extensively. The purpose of the diagram is to show how a user can move from one window to another along major, "application-meaningful" paths.

Figure 3-4 shows the basic elements of a windows navigation diagram.

Figure 3-5 shows an example of a windows navigation diagram. In this figure, the user arrives at a window on which she can modify a product price list. Selecting New from the File menu will take her to a

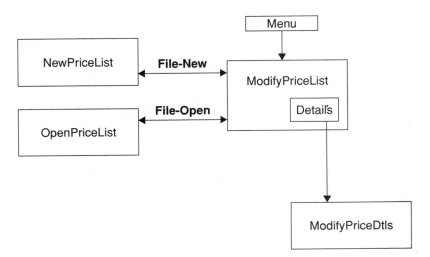

Figure 3-5 *Sample Windows Navigation Diagram*

window where she can start a new list; selecting Open from that menu will take her to a window where she can retrieve an existing list. Regardless of which path she takes, she must return to the main window, where she can press the Details button to bring up a "modify price details" window.

Whether you build a prototype, draw mockups, or use some other technique(s) to address the visual aspects of your system, it's very useful to link your screen designs to your use cases. You can do this manually or in the context of a visual modeling tool, such as Rational Rose (see Figure 3-6).

Think, again, in terms of a user manual. A screen shot appears, showing, for instance, your snazzy extra-wide scroll bars and unique button design. But the text doesn't say anything about that stuff—it just tells the reader what to do. For instance, here's what might appear in the user manual in connection with Figure 3-3:

1. Select the appropriate Trade Type.
2. Use the drop-down menu to choose the Investment involved in the trade you are entering.
3. Type the Ticket Number that appears on the paper ticket you are holding.
4. If you are satisfied with the entries you have made on this screen, click the Proceed button. Otherwise, click the Cancel button to return to the previous screen.

The coupling between the screen and the text is obvious, as is the similarity between this text and the use case text we've been presenting.

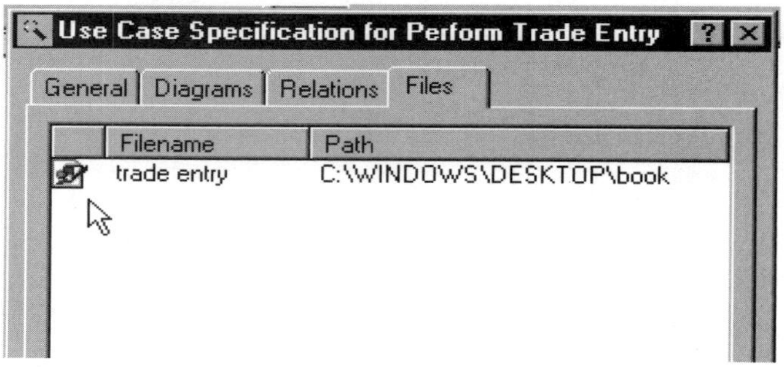

Figure 3-6 *Linking Files to Use Cases Within Rational Rose*

It's also true, though, that each piece can stand on its own. Just as a technical writer might choose to import that screen shot "by reference" instead of copying it directly into the manual, one might think of the use case model as incorporating the user interface model by reference.

I need to point out here that not only shouldn't your use case text include too many presentation details, but it should be relatively free of details about the fields on your screens, as well. *Field names* often match up directly with the *names of attributes on your domain classes*, which I talk about in the next chapter. The narrative of a use case should be event-response oriented, as in, "The system does this when the user does that."

Mining Your Legacy User Manuals for Use Cases

The basic principles I described in this section don't apply only to newly conceived systems. *If you're reengineering a legacy system, you can simply work from the user manual backward*. Look at the descriptions of the existing functionality. Then make changes based on how those functions will be performed in the new system. Instead of building a new manual from the ground up, you'll find yourself tearing the current manual down into its fundamental components, which will serve as the building blocks of your use case modeling.

For instance, suppose our example Portfolio Trading and Accounting system, which will have a GUI, was based on a system that had mainframe-style entry screens. Let's also suppose that the old trade entry screen for a bond trade involving a bond used function keys—F6 to go to a second entry screen that has other fields, for instance. In this case, the use case modeler would be able to replace the function key text with text that is less focused on the user interface and more focused on the desired system behavior.

 Whether you use prototyping, screen mockups, or the results of mining legacy user manuals, it's important that you do a thorough job *before* you start writing use case text. If you don't, you could end up spending a *lot* of extra time trying to pin down what your users expect to be doing with the new system.

ALERT! *Don't try to write use cases until you know what the users will actually be doing.*

Refining Use Cases

We'll now start tracking the evolution of a use case for our new system, which we'll call Perform Trade Entry.

Here's a first cut:

> The Assistant Trader (AT) uses a trade entry window to enter the original data for a trade. The system validates the data before processing the trade. The AT has the option of making changes to trade data later.

This captures the basic points, but it's rather terse. When it comes to writing text for use cases, expansive is much preferable to terse. Let's see how we can improve and build upon this text.

Once you have some text in place for a use case, it's time to refine it by making sure the sentences are clear and discrete, the verbs are strong, and the actors and potential domain objects are easily identifiable. (Later in this chapter, I will talk about updating your static model with the results of your use case analysis. This is another recurring theme within the ICONIX approach: The static model isn't really static until the system works.) You are also likely to be in continuous learning mode as work progresses with your users, so you'll have a chance to add new knowledge to your text along the way.

Suppose we decided to combine the order entry task, which we discussed in "Working Inward from a GUI to Identify Use Cases" (see page 41), and the trade entry task we outlined within Perform Trade Entry. Here's how we might expand that use case's text:

> The Assistant Trader (AT) uses an order entry window to enter the data for an order. The system ensures that the trade number that the AT entered is unique. Then the system determines what type of investment is going to be traded and brings up the appropriate trade entry window in response. The AT then uses that window to enter the original data for the associated trade. When the AT finishes making entries, the AT indicates that the trade is ready for processing. The system validates certain entries (for example, it makes sure the settlement date does not precede the trade date) and then processes the trade appropriately.

As we walk through this use case, we can quickly classify the various parts of speech in modeling terms. There is a human actor named *Assistant Trader*. We can recognize objects named *Trade* and *Investment* that are already part of our domain model. And there will also be some kind of *Trade Entry Window*.

Chapter 4 describes the process by which you classify the objects you identify via use case analysis as boundary objects, entity objects, and control objects. Sometimes, it's actually easier to draw a robustness diagram before writing use case text. Regardless of which comes first, though, you need to keep in mind that *you're not finished with a use case until the text and the robustness diagram match.*

Meanwhile, the latest version of Perform Trade Entry raises at least two questions.

1. What does "processing a trade" mean?
2. What happens if the AT does something wrong?

We'll deal with the first question when we come back to this use case in Chapter 5. The next section addresses the second question.

Basic and Alternate Courses of Action

A use case describes one or more *courses* through a user operation. The *basic* course must always be present; *alternate* courses are optional (but *not*, as we'll see, unimportant).

The **basic course of action** of a use case is the main start-to-finish path the user will follow, under normal circumstances (the "sunny day" scenario, in other words). For instance, within the Perform Trade Entry use case, all the text we have at this point is for the basic course, such as, "The system validates certain entries (for example, it makes sure the settlement date does not precede the trade date) and then processes the trade appropriately." There is an implicit assumption that the *Assistant Trader* has entered all the data for the given trade correctly—the date doesn't precede the current date, the price is expressed appropriately, and so forth.

An **alternate course of action** can represent an infrequently used path through the scenario, an exception, or an error condition. Here's an alternate course of action for Perform Trade Entry:

> If the validation fails, notify the user, highlight the erroneous values, and get new values from the user.

Basic courses of action are generally easier to identify and write text for. That doesn't mean, however, you should put off dealing with alternate courses until, say, detailed design. Far from it. In fact, all too often I've seen nasty errors of omission cause serious problems at that point in a project, when taking the time to write out alternate courses up front would have saved the team considerable grief.

It's been my experience that when important alternate courses of action are not uncovered until coding and debugging, *the programmer responsible for writing or fixing the code tends to treat them in ways that are most convenient for him or her*. Needless to say, this isn't healthy for a project.

Although some authors encourage the use of voluminous use case templates, here's what I recommend to *every one* of my clients:

1. *Create a use case template* that has areas labeled Basic Course and Alternate Courses. Don't put anything else in there; it'll just distract you.
2. *Ask "What happens?"* This will get the basic course of action started.
3. *Ask "And then what happens?"* Keep asking that question until you have all the details of your basic course on paper.
4. *Be relentless.* "What *else* can happen? Are there *any* other things that can happen? Are you *sure*?" Keep asking *those* questions until you have a rich set of alternate courses written down. Trust me: Grief at this point is much easier to take than grief during, say, integration testing.

The goal is *not* to construct an elegant use case model; the goal is to account for *everything* the user might do.

You'll review this material before you finish use case modeling; you'll review it *again* during robustness analysis (discussed in the next chapter); and you'll review it *once more* during interaction modeling (see Chapter 5). This may seem excessive, but keep this in mind: The more well-defined the system behavior, the easier it's going to be to build the system.

Factoring Out Commonality in Usage

You can use several mechanisms to factor out common usage, such as error handling, from sets of use cases. This is usually a good thing to do, because breaking usage down to atomic levels will make your analysis effort easier, and save you lots of time when you're drawing sequence diagrams, too.

Constructs from the UML and OML

The UML offers three of these mechanisms.

1. **Generalization** works the same way with use cases as it does with regular classes: The child use case inherits the behavior and meaning of the parent use case, and so forth. The notation is the same, too. (See "Build Generalization Relationships" on page 21.)

2. The **includes** relationship (previously known as **uses**) involves one use case making full use of another use case. This goes to the issue of reuse, which is a prime objective of use case modeling, since it helps us factor out commonality. This construct is predefined as a **stereotype** that you can add to a use case diagram; you can also do what I do, and put "includes" as the label on the arrow.

3. The **extends** relationship allows the modeler to insert one use case into another use case, thus "extending" the second use case. The main idea behind this construct is that you can use it to show optional system behavior, or behavior that's executed only under certain conditions. This is also predefined as a stereotype.

Because the UML defines a use case as one form of a class, use case generalization is certainly a technically viable concept. However, I don't generalize use cases, because generalization is most useful for building elaborate structures dominated by abstract use cases.

 These structures are great for organizing requirements that aren't linked directly to design elements, but we're talking about getting from use cases to code, so I won't talk anymore about use case generalization.

ALERT! *Don't spend weeks building elaborate, elegant use case models that you can't design from.*

On the other hand, I *do* have something to say about *includes* and *extends*. Note that in the following discussion, I refer to the *includes* construct as *uses*, which is what *includes* was called in Jacobson's original book and in early versions of the UML.

In my years of teaching use case driven development, I have yet to come across a situation in which I have needed more than one mechanism for factoring out commonality. (I maintain this despite a seemingly endless debate about *uses* versus *extends* that is probably still going on, as you read this—albeit now in the form of *includes* versus *extends*—within the Object Technology User Group [OTUG]. See the appendix for more on this subject.)

 I also think, however, that having two similar constructs is worse than having only one. It's just too easy to get confused—and bogged down—when you try to use both.

ALERT! *Don't spin your wheels worrying about whether to use includes, extends, and/or uses.*

Even in the face of the terminology change within the UML, which doesn't address the fundamental problem, I find myself now leaning toward concepts from the Open Modeling Language (OML) called **invokes** and **precedes**. These would take the form of user-defined stereotypes on your use case diagrams.

The idea behind *invokes* is that one use case invokes another one in the same basic manner that a function invokes a peer function. You use *precedes* to indicate that one use case needs to precede another within a logical sequence.

The appendix offers samples of the long-running and often bitter debate between the advocates of *uses* and *extends* and the folks who are happy with *invokes* and *precedes*. Meanwhile, I use *invokes* and *precedes* in a couple of places later in this chapter.

One reason I like to see *precedes* on a use case diagram is that it helps keep the focus on what's inside the given use case. It's all too easy to get distracted by how you get there (that is, the **precondition**) and/or by what happens once you leave (the **postcondition**).

 Once again, let me encourage you not to worry about adhering to the gospel of the UML when you do a project. Instead, you should use whatever will work well in a given situation.

Pick one of the mechanisms I've described here, or another one that you know about, and *use it consistently*. Nor should you insist on using long and complex use case templates just because they appeared in a book or article.

ALERT! *Don't waste time with long and involved use case templates.*

Consider the statements I just made as warnings about ways you might build up resistance to doing use cases, which offers an excuse to ditch modeling altogether—and we all know what happens then. (Hint: "The code's written, so I guess we're done!")

Back to Our Example

The current text for the basic course of action of our Perform Trade Entry use case, which appears at the bottom of page 46, is reasonable, but it's still pretty generic, and it also lends itself to factoring. Let's see how we can work with this text to create additional use cases, each of which is more specific—and thus more useful—for our example system. This is all part of our ongoing exploration of how the users will use the new system.

For starters, it turns out that buy trades and sell trades have certain features in common, as well as some different characteristics.

This leads us to do two things with Perform Trade Entry.

1. Create new use cases called Enter Buy Trade and Enter Sell Trade. These will capture the unique characteristics of the different types of trades.

2. Create a use case called Perform Order Entry that *precedes* either of the other new use cases. This will include the user behavior associated with the order entry task we originally decided to lump in with the trade entry task.

Figure 3-7 shows the results of performing these steps, in a use case diagram.

We can write the following text for the basic course of action of Perform Order Entry.

> The Assistant Trader (AT) uses an order entry window to enter the data for an order that involves a buy or sell trade. First, the AT specifies the trade type. Then the AT selects the

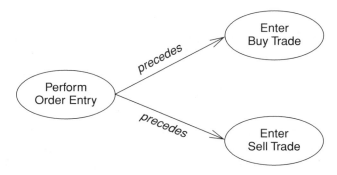

Figure 3-7 *Use Case Factoring*

investment involved in the order from a list of available investments. The AT also enters the ticket number that appears on the paper ticket for the order.

Once all the necessary data is in place, the AT presses a button to tell the system to process the order and bring up the appropriate type of trade entry window. The AT uses that window to enter the primary data for the trade connected with the new order.

The text for one alternate course of action is:

If the ticket number already exists, the system prompts the AT to enter a new ticket number.

Here is an attempt at another alternate course:

If the investment associated with an order is not present in the system, the AT brings up an investment entry window. The AT defines the appropriate information for that investment, and the system validates that information (for example, it ensures that the identifier appears in a known format). Once the system has accepted the investment definition, it returns the AT to the order entry window.

The problem with this text as an alternate course of action is that it introduces a new window that will likely have a number of different kinds of fields, in contrast with, say, an error dialog box. In situations like this, it's best to break out the text into another new use case. For our example, we'll call this new use case Define Investment.

We can use the preceding text as the basic course for Define Investment. For our alternate course, we can lift the text from our now-obsolete Perform Trade Entry use case:

> If the validation fails, notify the user, highlight the erroneous values, and get new values from the user.

With this new use case in place, the second alternate course for Perform Order Entry then becomes:

> If the investment associated with the order has not yet been defined, the system invokes the Define Investment use case.

In keeping with the idea of continuous improvement, the text for the basic course of action for Perform Order Entry enables us to compress the basic course of action for our new Enter Buy Trade use case. If we assume that the user wants to enter a trade that involves a purchase of bonds, the text might read:

> The Assistant Trader (AT) uses a Bond Trade Entry window to enter the primary values for the trade. The system validates both general trade values and bond-specific values (for instance, it makes sure the coupon rate is "reasonable") before processing the trade.

And we can reuse the alternate course for Define Investment as the alternative course for Enter Buy Trade:

> If the validation fails, notify the user, highlight the erroneous values, and get new values from the user.

At this point, we could define another new use case for error handling. Given the different sorts of business rules associated with *Trade*s and *Investments*, which we'll have to address somewhere down the line (during design), we won't go that route. Note, though, that it's always a good idea to keep your eye open for opportunities to simplify and clarify.

Before we proceed with the last two use cases that comprise our example system's use case model, notice that all the use case text in this section is in ***present tense and active voice***, and that the sentences are precise and clear.

This is the kind of text you would expect to see in a user manual. In fact, it's often a good idea to bring a technical writer into the process at this stage for that very reason. A seasoned tech writer has a good feel for how to capture the essence of what a user wants to do. (Also, tech writers are not likely to be in a hurry to cut code.)

The text for the basic course of action for our new Enter Sell Trade use case, which is also *preceded* by Perform Order Entry, comprises the basic course text for Enter Buy Trade with an extra sentence in the middle to account for a key difference between buy and sell trades:

> The Assistant Trader (AT) uses a Bond Trade Entry window to enter the primary values for the trade. As part of this task, the system brings up a pairoff window, which the AT uses to select one or more buy trades to "pair off" with the new sell trade.
>
> The system validates both general trade values and bond-specific values (for instance, it makes sure that the coupon rate is "reasonable") before processing the trade.

I mentioned earlier that buys and sells have some common features. Therefore, we can use Enter Buy Trade's alternate course for Enter Sell Trade:

> If the validation fails, notify the user, highlight the erroneous values, and get new values from the user.

The last use case in our model has its roots in the following sentence from our original attempt at writing text for Perform Trade Entry: "The AT has the option of making changes to trade data later." (That one almost slipped through the cracks! *Attention to detail is crucial!*)

This is the basic course of action for Perform Trade Adjustment:

> The Assistant Trader (AT) enters a trade number on a trade adjustment window. The system finds the data for the trade and displays it on the window. The AT can edit certain fields, such as the commission amount, but not others, such as the trade date and the quantity.
>
> After the AT has finished making entries, the AT submits the trade for processing. The system validates certain entries and then processes the trade adjustment appropriately.

The following are Perform Trade Adjustment's alternate courses:

> If the system cannot find the ticket number the AT entered, the system prompts the AT to enter a new ticket number.

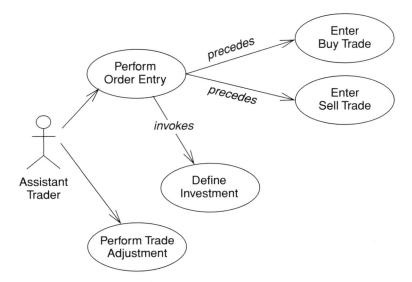

Figure 3-8 *Use Case Diagram for Example System*

> If the validation fails, notify the user, highlight the erroneous values, and get new values from the user.

Figure 3-8 shows the full use case diagram for our example system as it now stands.

Use Case Packages

In the UML, a **package** is a grouping of related elements, such as classes. I like to group use cases into packages, primarily because these packages form logical boundaries for dividing work among sub-teams. A good rule to follow is: *Each package should correspond with a chapter, or at least a major section, in your user manual*.

Figure 3-9 is a **package diagram** that shows two packages for our example system: one that contains the use cases we've been looking at, and another that holds use cases that might appear in another part of the system. Note that you can put a class diagram in a package, too; a

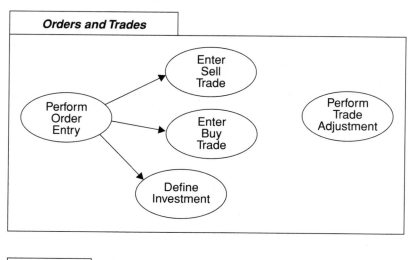

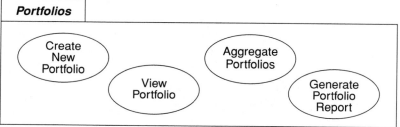

Figure 3-9 *Package Diagram for Example System*

package can contain any other element of the UML (including another package).

Use Cases and Requirements

The relationship between requirements and use cases is the subject of much discussion—well, argument—in the object-oriented community. My take on it can be summarized as follows.

- A use case describes a unit of behavior.
- A requirement describes a law that governs behavior.
- A use case can satisfy one or more functional requirements.
- A functional requirement may be satisfied by one or more use cases.

Note my use of the words *may* and *functional*. A system will have its share of functional requirements, but it will also have other types of requirements, such as those involving performance and maintainability, that won't map well to use cases. I explore different types of requirements and talk about the importance of traceability in connection with those requirements in Chapter 7.

Wrapping Up Use Case Modeling

You should feel comfortable proceeding to the next phases of the development process when you've achieved the following goals of use case modeling:

1. You've built use cases that together account for *all* of the desired functionality of the system.
2. You've produced clear and concise written descriptions of the basic course of action, along with appropriate alternate courses of action, for each use case.
3. You've factored out scenarios common to more than one use case, using the *precedes* and *invokes* constructs (or whichever constructs you're most comfortable using).

Figure 3-10 and Figure 3-11 show the tasks I discussed in this chapter.

I talk about requirements at some length in Chapter 7. As I indicate in Figure 3-10, you should perform at least a preliminary review of your requirements with your users before you proceed with robustness analysis, the subject of the next chapter. There's no sense heading into preliminary design unless you're still on track with your customers!

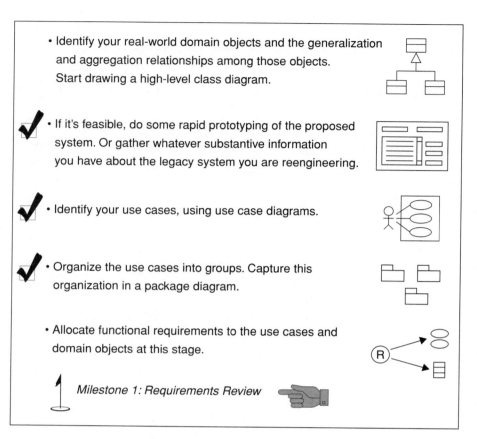

- Identify your real-world domain objects and the generalization and aggregation relationships among those objects. Start drawing a high-level class diagram.

- If it's feasible, do some rapid prototyping of the proposed system. Or gather whatever substantive information you have about the legacy system you are reengineering.

- Identify your use cases, using use case diagrams.

- Organize the use cases into groups. Capture this organization in a package diagram.

- Allocate functional requirements to the use cases and domain objects at this stage.

Milestone 1: Requirements Review

Figure 3-10 *Requirements Analysis Checkpoint 2*

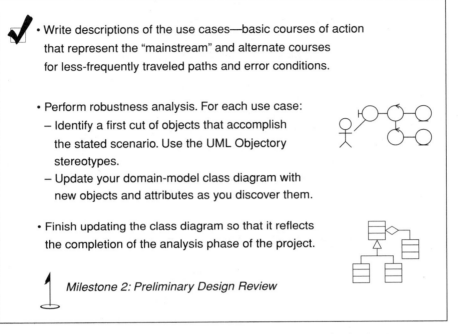

- Write descriptions of the use cases—basic courses of action that represent the "mainstream" and alternate courses for less-frequently traveled paths and error conditions.

- Perform robustness analysis. For each use case:
  - Identify a first cut of objects that accomplish the stated scenario. Use the UML Objectory stereotypes.
  - Update your domain-model class diagram with new objects and attributes as you discover them.

- Finish updating the class diagram so that it reflects the completion of the analysis phase of the project.

Milestone 2: Preliminary Design Review

Figure 3-11 *Analysis and Preliminary Design Checkpoint 1*

Top 10 Mistakes to Avoid When Writing Use Cases

10. Write functional requirements instead of usage scenario text.

9. Describe attributes and methods rather than usage.

8. Write the use cases too tersely.

7. Divorce yourself completely from the user interface.

6. Avoid explicit names for your boundary objects.

5. Write using a perspective other than the user's, in passive voice.

4. Describe only user interactions; ignore system responses.

3. Omit text for alternative courses of action.

2. Focus on something other than what's "inside" a use case, such as how you get there (precondition) or what happens afterward (postcondition).

1. Spend a month deciding whether to use includes or extends.

Chapter 4

Robustness Analysis

Ivar Jacobson introduced the concept of **robustness analysis** to the world of OO in 1991. It involves analyzing the narrative text of each of your use cases and identifying a first-guess set of objects that will participate in the use case, then classifying these objects into the following three types of objects:

1. **Boundary objects**, which actors use in communicating with the system
2. **Entity objects**, which are usually objects from the domain model
3. **Control objects**, which serve as the "glue" between boundary objects and entity objects

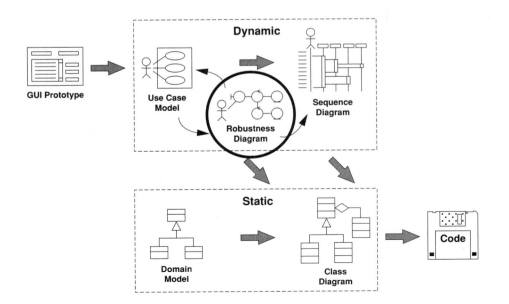

Note that boundary objects are what used to be called interface objects. The amigos changed the name because of conflicts with the term *interface* as it's used elsewhere (for instance, in Java and COM).

This simple but highly useful technique serves as a crucial link between analysis—the *what*—and design—the *how* (see Figure 4-1).

I suspect that robustness analysis started as an informal pencil and paper technique, and that Jacobson and his colleagues incorporated it into his Objectory process once they realized how well it works.

The amigos continue to point out the rather large analysis/design gap, as evidenced by this passage from *The Unified Modeling Language User Guide* (Addison-Wesley, 1998):

> In software, the Achilles heel of structured analysis techniques is the fact that there is a basic disconnect between its analysis model and the system's design model. *Failing to bridge this chasm causes the system as conceived and the system as built to diverge over time.* [Emphasis added.] In object-oriented systems, it is possible to connect all the nearly independent views of a system into one semantic whole.

Unfortunately, robustness analysis is not part of the UML proper. Rather, it makes its appearance as part of Rational's *UML Objectory Process-Specific Extensions* document. In this document, the three types of objects take the form of **stereotypes**, which are ways to classify elements so that they behave in ways the UML doesn't formally define.

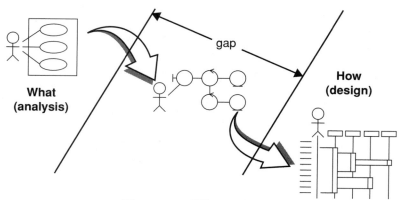

What
(analysis)

gap

How
(design)

Figure 4-1 *What vs. How*

Much to my dismay, the trend continues with the Rational Unified Process (RUP), into which robustness analysis seems to be disappearing.

I'm not sure why the amigos chose to skip preliminary design, but regardless, I will explain why robustness analysis is so critical and how to do it the way Jacobson intended.

Key Roles of Robustness Analysis

Robustness analysis plays several essential roles within the Unified Object Modeling approach.

- **Sanity check**—Robustness analysis helps you make sure your use case text is correct and that you haven't specified system behavior that's unreasonable—or impossible—given the set of objects you have to work with.
- **Completeness check**—Robustness analysis helps you make sure those use cases address all the necessary alternate courses of action.
- **Ongoing discovery of objects**—You may have missed some objects during domain modeling.
- **Preliminary design**—See the previous section.

Sanity Check

The diagrams you draw during this phase graphically depict the flow within your use cases. In fact, as we'll see later in the chapter, *you should replace the generic nouns in your use case text with the proper names of objects that appear in your robustness diagrams.* In so doing, you're forced to review the use case text. In most cases, you'll want to refine it further before you move on to the next use case.

This refinement changes the nature of the use case text from a pure user manual perspective to a usage description *in the context of the object model.* As we'll see, this is the magic formula you need to build useful sequence diagrams.

This iteration happens so frequently, in my experience, that we made robustness analysis an integral part of writing use case text. This is one way our approach contrasts with that of Jacobson, who made robustness

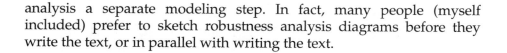

analysis a separate modeling step. In fact, many people (myself included) prefer to sketch robustness analysis diagrams before they write the text, or in parallel with writing the text.

Completeness Check

Since robustness diagrams carry certain conventions—for instance, actors should be connected only to boundary objects (see Figure 4-3 on page 69 for the full set of rules)—iterating through your use cases in this context will help you produce use case text that adheres to some well-defined guidelines.

For example, you should refer to GUI elements (a common form of boundary objects) by name and describe how the actors use each element. This leads to the identification of the various windows, or screens, by name, which is a useful thing to do earlier rather than later.

Because so much depends on the use cases, it's worth the effort to make sure they're complete and written in an appropriate style. A more or less uniform text style is critical to reviewability and also in terms of heading off potential problems later in a project, when no one wants to try to figure out what this or that writer meant.

As I mentioned earlier, robustness analysis, which is basically preliminary design, is a very useful step between abstract analysis and detailed design.

I recommend you use sequence diagrams as the next design step (see Chapter 5). If you do a proper robustness analysis, you'll find it much easier to address the sequence diagrams. From a mechanical standpoint, this is because you can copy the names of boundary objects and entity objects directly to get your sequence diagrams started. From a productivity standpoint, if you skip robustness analysis, you run a risk of not discovering all the objects you may need, and that risk is associated with some potentially serious consequences.

"Control objects" occasionally end up as objects in the static model, but more often, you end up converting them into operations on entity objects and/or boundary objects. This means that you can use your sequence diagrams to get the designers focused on the very important task of doing a good, clean allocation of behavior (that is, deciding which methods belong to which objects). In my experience, *the time spent drawing robustness diagrams is invariably made up three- or four-fold in time saved in drawing sequence diagrams.*

Object Identification

Because this is the stage of the process in which you refine the proper names you started assigning your objects during domain modeling, you can also address naming discrepancies and conflicts before they cause serious problems. For instance, one team may call something a *Cash Drawer*; another team will refer to the same thing as a *Cash Dispenser*. The resulting mess is not much fun to clean up as the teams compare notes. A good rule to follow is: *Use the names from the domain model for your entity objects.*

I discussed reuse in the previous chapter. Robustness analysis allows you to make a reuse pass through the entire use case model before you commit any use cases to the design. Looking for reuse possibilities also helps you identify objects you missed during domain modeling.

Identifying commonality is a good reason to spend time on domain modeling early in a project. We start building what one might call an *object glossary* by looking first for the names of our entity objects in the domain model. Later, as we uncover new entity objects missed during the initial domain modeling effort, we add these new objects to our domain model. This forms a major part of the continuous refinement that occurs from the domain model to the detailed static model, from which we can write code.

By the time we finish robustness analysis, we should have identified most of the major entity objects (or domain classes) in the system— and we've done this *before* the first sequence diagram is drawn. This is very important, because allocating behavior across an incomplete set of objects is likely to be messy. (Translation: Rework and more rework and associated slipping of schedules.)

Preliminary Design

Sequence diagrams are fairly involved and tedious to draw because they are densely packed with information. Robustness diagrams are much simpler and easier to read, and they can be drawn and redrawn relatively quickly as refinement occurs.

Looking down the road at partitioning, the Boundary–Entity–Control trio maps well to the Model–View–Controller construct that comes from Smalltalk, and it also lends itself handsomely to traditional client/server implementation in the form of GUI–Repository–Logic.

All things considered, the work products of robustness analysis, even though the diagrams themselves are more or less throwaways, come in awfully handy.

 The concept of throwaway diagrams is useful in connection with preliminary design; it is *not* a useful concept when it comes to detailed design. Sequence diagrams, which I discuss in the next chapter, are the appropriate place for detailed design.

ALERT! *Don't try to do detailed design on robustness diagrams.*

More About Robustness Analysis Object Types

Boundary objects are the objects in the new system with which the actors (for instance, the users) will be interacting. These frequently include windows, screens, dialogs, and menus.

If you have a prototype in place, you can see what many of your primary boundary objects will be. You can also easily pick boundary objects out of your use case text. The window navigation diagram I discussed in Chapter 3 can also be a useful source of boundary objects.

Looking ahead, you should associate what one might call local validation logic with boundary objects. This includes any kind of error checking that doesn't require an object to interact with other objects in the system. For instance, in the context of a Trade Entry window, the system will need to make sure the trade settlement date follows the trade execution date, that neither date has a 13 in the month portion, and so forth. For now, these should take the form of control objects associated with your boundary objects; we'll defer the decision about how to assign the logic until we do our sequence diagrams.

You'll use some of these boundary objects in addressing alternate courses of action within your use cases. For example, you might have warning and error dialog boxes that will appear separate from your entry windows. I will introduce some of these kinds of boundary objects to our example later in the chapter; Chapter 5 contains further information.

Speaking of alternate courses, you should check—again—to see whether you have all of them in place while you're identifying new objects for them. One can never hear it too often: Nailing down the required behavior of the system *before* starting design is considerably less costly, in tangible *and* intangible terms, than identifying it later.

Entity objects often map to the database tables and files that hold the information that needs to "outlive" use case execution. Many of your entity objects will come from your domain model, which I discussed in Chapter 2.

I tend to think of many entity objects as "dumb servers." They should store data, fetch data, and perform fundamental kinds of computations that don't change very often. The simpler and more generic your entity objects, the greater your prospects of reusing them in other projects.

In our example system, *GLAccount* qualifies as an entity object. Our users will define their chart of accounts and the rules associated with general ledger posting soon after they get hold of the finished system. That chart and those rules won't be likely to change after that.

Control objects—which I call **controllers**—embody much of the application logic. They serve as the connecting tissue between the users and the stored data. This is where you capture your (frequently changing) business rules and policies, with the idea that you can *localize changes* to these objects without disrupting your user interface or your database schema down the line.

Unlike boundary objects and entity objects, controllers are not necessarily meant to endure as stand-alone classes as you proceed with design. You're likely to find yourself converting many controllers into methods associated with interface objects and entity objects. *Control objects serve as* **placeholders** *to make sure you don't forget any functionality and system behavior required by your use cases.*

Performing Robustness Analysis

Figure 4-2 shows how you represent these three types of objects on robustness diagrams.

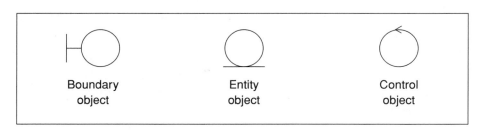

Figure 4-2 *Robustness Diagram Symbols*

Before we go back to the example system again, I'd like to offer two guiding principles.

1. I like to see a small number (say, between two and five) of controllers per average use case. If you have only one controller per use case, you're likely to have a lot of very small use cases.

    A number between five and 10 is generally workable. But if you have more than 10 control objects in a given use case, you should consider splitting it.

2. Arrows can go in one or both directions between different types of objects. An arrow pointing from a boundary object to a control object indicates that the former is signalling the latter to perform. Or there might be a two-headed arrow between a control object and an entity object, signifying that they read from each other and write to each other.

    Note, however, that you need to use only one type of arrowhead, which is *not* the case on several types of UML diagrams.

    Unlike arrows on sequence diagrams, arrows on robustness diagrams *don't* represent software messages; rather, they simply indicate logical associations. Because you won't code from these diagrams, focus on the logical flow of your use case and worry about the directions of arrows later, in your sequence diagrams.

Another benefit of robustness analysis is that it helps enforce a common noun-verb-noun style of writing use cases across a design team.

Figure 4-3 shows what you can and cannot do on a robustness diagram.

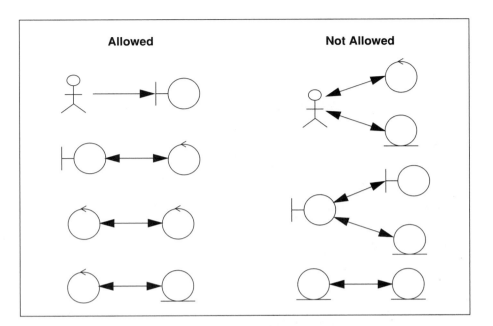

Figure 4-3 *Robustness Diagram Rules*

We can capture the essence of this diagram with four statements.

1. Actors can talk only to boundary objects.
2. Boundary objects can talk only to controllers and actors.
3. Entity objects can also talk only to controllers.
4. Controllers can talk to both boundary objects and controllers, but not to actors.

Now let's revisit our budding example system.

Figure 4-4 contains the basic and alternate courses of action for two of the use cases we wrote in Chapter 3.

These use cases will be our primary source for boundary objects in the robustness diagrams we'll see shortly. The text is also a rich source of entity objects, because we made a point of connecting it with our domain model while we were writing it. We'll also be able to identify some controllers we need.

Perform Order Entry

Basic Course: The Assistant Trader (AT) uses an order entry window to enter the data for an order that involves a buy or sell trade. First, the AT specifies the trade type. Then the AT selects the investment involved in the order from a list of available investments. The AT also enters the ticket number that appears on the paper ticket for the order.

Once all of the necessary data is in place, the AT presses a button to tell the system to process the order and bring up the appropriate type of trade entry window. The AT will use that window to enter the primary data for the trade connected with the new order.

Alternate Course: If the ticket number already exists, the system prompts the AT to enter a new ticket number.

Alternate Course: If the investment associated with the given order has not yet been defined, the system invokes the Define Investment use case.

Enter Buy Trade

Basic Course: The Assistant Trader (AT) uses a bond trade entry window to enter the primary values for the trade. The system validates both general trade values and bond-specific values (for instance, it makes sure the coupon rate is "reasonable") before processing the trade.

Alternate Course: If the validation fails, notify the user, highlight the erroneous values, and get new values from the user.

Figure 4-4 *Use Cases for Example System*

Let's analyze the Perform Order Entry use case and come up with details we'll need for our robustness diagram.

- Because the value the AT specifies for the trade type will lead to the system invoking either of two other use cases (Enter Buy Trade or Enter Sell Trade), let's show this sub-task as the last one the AT performs on the Order Entry window.
- That window has a list box that shows the available investments. Underneath that, we'll need the actual list, as well as some kind of control object that sits in the middle.
- The first alternate course of action says that the system needs to check for a duplicate ticket number. So we've discovered our first new object: a **trade list**. We also need controllers that get the num-

ber the AT enters and check that number against the list. If the number is a duplicate, the system will bring up a prompt for the AT to enter a different number. If it's not a duplicate, the system will go ahead and create a new *Order* object.

- The second alternate course tells us that Perform Order Entry might invoke Define Investment. This calls for a boundary object via which this will happen. We also need another new entity object: an **investment list**.

Figure 4-5 shows a robustness diagram that might result from this analysis. Pay particular attention to the middle note. This diagram has a fundamental flaw related to one of the bullet points above, which we'll talk about in the next chapter.

A comparable analysis of Enter Buy Trade goes like this:

- We need to show that the *Order* object that Perform Order Entry created before invoking Enter Buy Trade is what creates the Bond Trade Entry window and the new *Trade* object in its initial form. (We'll have a control object that retrieves the AT's entries and puts them into *Trade*.)
- The use case calls for a feedback loop, which involves the window and a "validate" control object, to address the alternate course.
- It's time to be more specific about what "processing a trade" means, so let's bring in a **trade queue** (this is our second new object) and an actor that represents the back office system.

Figure 4-6 shows a (correct) robustness diagram for Enter Buy Trade.

Now, let's rewrite the text for the two use cases we're highlighting in this chapter to reflect our newly captured details.

Here is the new basic course of action for Perform Order Entry:

> The system displays an Order Entry window. The AT first selects the investment involved in the order from a list of available investments. The AT then enters the ticket number that appears on the paper ticket for the order, and also specifies whether the trade is a buy or a sell. The system verifies that the ticket number is not a duplicate; if the number is unique, the system creates a new order. When the AT chooses to proceed, the system brings up the appropriate trade entry window, which the AT uses to enter the primary data for the trade.

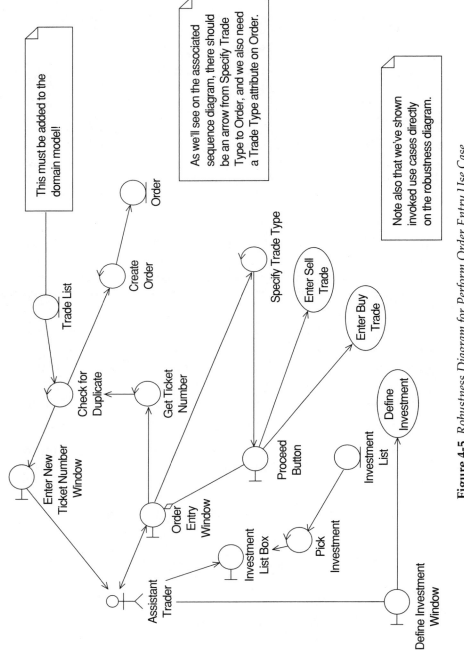

This must be added to the domain model!

As we'll see on the associated sequence diagram, there should be an arrow from Specify Trade Type to Order, and we also need a Trade Type attribute on Order.

Note also that we've shown invoked use cases directly on the robustness diagram.

Figure 4-5 *Robustness Diagram for Perform Order Entry Use Case*

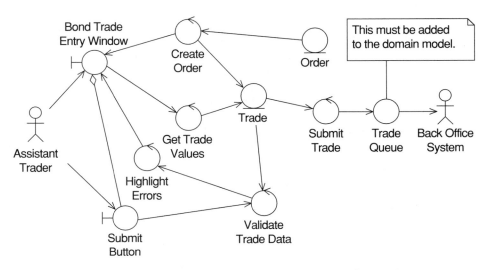

Figure 4-6 *Robustness Diagram for Enter Buy Trade Use Case*

The improved alternate courses are:

> If the ticket number already exists in the Trade List, the system prompts the AT to enter a new ticket number.

> If the investment associated with the order does not appear in the Investment List, the system invokes the Define Investment use case.

Compare this with the intermediate text on page 51, and then ask yourself which text would be easier to design from!

Let's do the same exercise for Enter Buy Trade. This is the new basic course:

> The system creates a new trade with the ticket number attached to the order. It also brings up a Bond Trade Entry window. The AT uses this window to enter the appropriate values for the trade. When the AT chooses to submit the trade, the system validates both general trade values and bond-specific values (for instance, it makes sure the coupon rate is "reasonable") before processing the trade. If the trade passes all validation tests, the system submits it to the Trade Queue, from which the trade is later sent to the Back Office System to be cleared and processed further.

Because we didn't learn anything new about Enter Buy Trade's alternate course, we can leave that one intact:

> If the validation fails, notify the user, highlight the erroneous values, and get new values from the user.

I strongly recommend that you have peer review of all of your use case text and robustness diagrams. Each reviewer should be able to do the following for each use case.

- Read the course of action.
- Trace his or her finger along the associations on the corresponding robustness diagram.
- See a clear match between text and picture.

You're not done writing a use case until you can pass this simple test.

When you've reached that point for your entire set of use cases, the next step—drawing sequence diagrams—will be easier for you to perform than if you were starting from your use case text alone.

Updating Your Domain (Static) Model

You ***must*** update your domain model (see Figure 4-7) before you can consider yourself done with robustness analysis and ready to move on to interaction modeling.

In fact, the best thing you can do is ***continuously refine your static model*** while you work through your use cases during robustness analysis.

The new objects you discovered while you were drawing all those robustness diagrams and talking about them with your customers need to go onto your class diagrams *now*, not later. This is also the right time to add some key attributes to your more significant classes.

Figure 4-8 shows an expanded view of the feedback path between the robustness model and the static model.

At this stage of your exploration of the dynamic model, several things happen that together accelerate the evolution of the initial (problem space) domain model toward a final (solution space) class model.

- As we put our use case in the context of a use case diagram, and we write and refine our text for its basic and alternate courses, we *discover new entity objects*. (We've found three so far in our example

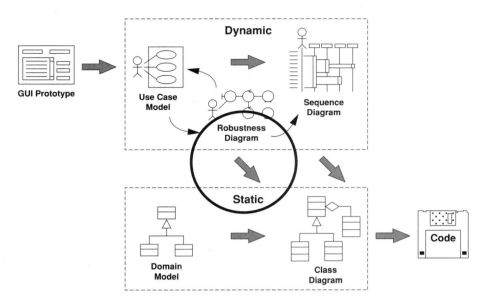

Figure 4-7 *Updating the Domain Model as Part of Robustness Analysis*

system: *TradeList*, *TradeQueue*, and *InvestmentList*.) That is, we first try to find domain classes with suitable names and use those names for the entities we need for our use case. Sometimes, during robustness analysis, we find that we're missing entities. As we add them to the robustness diagram, *we need to also add them to the domain model*.

- As we introduce windows and screens—in the form of boundary objects—to our robustness diagrams, we begin to **trace data** associated with those objects back to the entity objects from which the data comes and/or to which it goes. The natural result of that tracing is the *addition of attributes* to the classes in the domain model.

- Rigorous robustness analysis, with continuous reference back to the use case being analyzed, enables a *check for completeness*: a robustness diagram isn't done until the basic course and all alternate courses are represented. (Yes, you *do* need to ask that question again.)

- We *itemize all the required behavior of the use case* in the form of control objects (controllers). This involves taking the user manual view and identifying all the logical functions that must occur, then massaging the narrative of the use case text into a straightforward

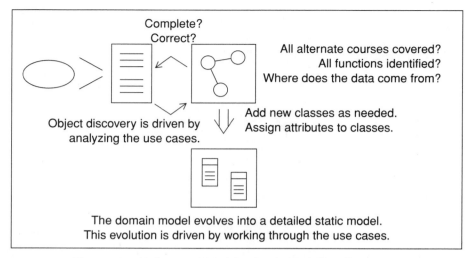

Complete?
Correct?

All alternate courses covered?
All functions identified?
Where does the data come from?

Object discovery is driven by
analyzing the use cases.

Add new classes as needed.
Assign attributes to classes.

The domain model evolves into a detailed static model.
This evolution is driven by working through the use cases.

Figure 4-8 *Robustness Model—Static Model Feedback Loop*

noun-verb-noun format. This format will allow us to *check for correctness* when we embark upon detailed design, by ensuring that we don't forget any behavior while we're doing the design.

The robustness diagram, then, serves as something of a "booster-stage engine" that gets the process of driving the use cases forward into an object-oriented design off the ground. Like the booster stage of a rocket, the robustness diagram can safely be discarded once it has served its purpose.

 In other words, robustness analysis is a tool that helps us discover objects, allocate attributes, and check the use case text for completeness and correctness. But once we've accomplished the overall mission, we don't need to maintain the work product. It's a means to an end, not an end in itself.

ALERT! *Don't waste time perfecting your robustness diagrams as your design evolves.*

We can see how this feedback loop works with regard to our example by making note of the three objects we discovered during our robustness analysis of Enter Buy Trade and Perform Trade Entry: *Investment List*, *Trade List*, and *Trade Queue*.

Figure 4-9 and Figure 4-10 together reflect the results of robustness analysis on the key elements of our example's static model.

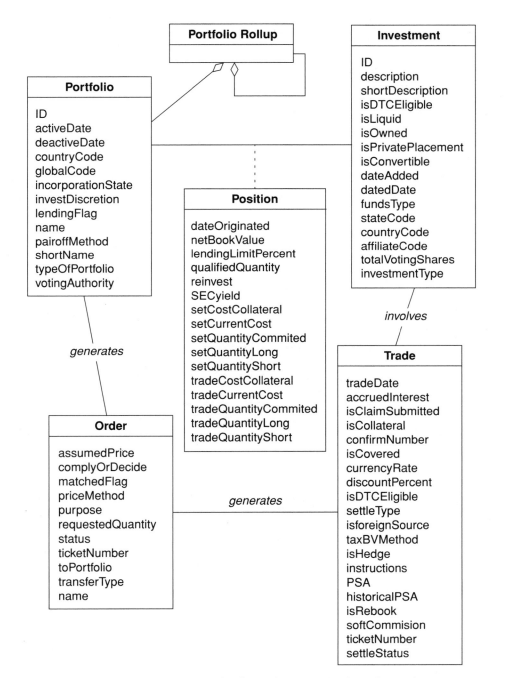

Figure 4-9 *Static Model After Robustness Analysis (Part 1)*

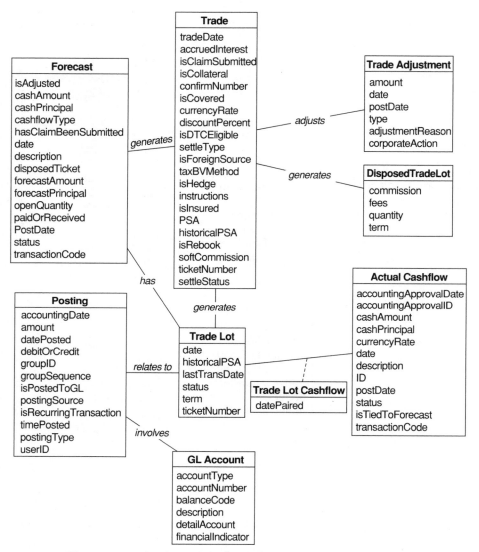

Figure 4-10 *Static Model After Robustness Analysis (Part 2)*

Wrapping Up Robustness Analysis

Figure 4-11 shows the tasks I discussed in this chapter. It also reminds you about the last thing you have to do before you proceed with detailed design, which is the subject of the next chapter.

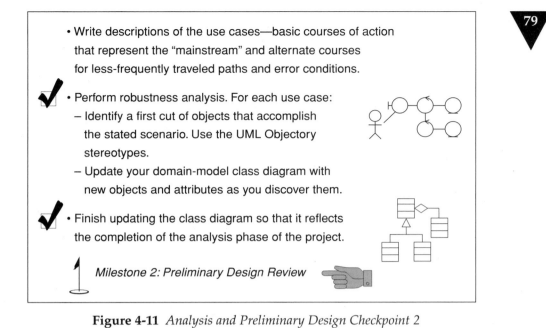

- Write descriptions of the use cases—basic courses of action that represent the "mainstream" and alternate courses for less-frequently traveled paths and error conditions.

- Perform robustness analysis. For each use case:
  - Identify a first cut of objects that accomplish the stated scenario. Use the UML Objectory stereotypes.
  - Update your domain-model class diagram with new objects and attributes as you discover them.

- Finish updating the class diagram so that it reflects the completion of the analysis phase of the project.

Milestone 2: Preliminary Design Review

Figure 4-11 *Analysis and Preliminary Design Checkpoint 2*

Top 10 Benefits of Robustness Analysis

10. *It forces you to write your use cases using a consistent style.*

9. *It forces you to write your use cases in the correct voice.*

8. *It provides sanity and completeness checks for the use cases.*

7. *It allows you apply syntax rules (for instance, "Actors talk only to boundary objects") to your use cases.*

6. *Robustness diagrams are quicker to draw and easier to read than sequence diagrams.*

5. *It helps you partition objects within a Model–View–Controller paradigm.*

4. *It helps you layer objects in a GUI–Logic–Repository framework for client/server systems.*

3. *It allows a reuse pass across all your use cases before you begin design.*

2. *It provides traceability between what the system does (use cases) and how the system works (sequence diagrams), using a conceptual object view.*

1. *It plugs the semantic gap between analysis (use cases) and design (sequence diagrams).*

Chapter 5

Interaction Modeling

When you finish with domain modeling and robustness analysis, you have uncovered most of your problem space objects and assigned some attributes to them. You have defined static relationships among the objects on your high-level class diagram, and a few dynamic relationships on your robustness diagrams. These represent fairly broad brush strokes. Now it's time to design how your software will really work (in other words, to define the solution to your problem). **Interaction modeling** is the phase in which you build the threads that weave your objects together and enable you to start seeing how your new system will perform useful behavior.

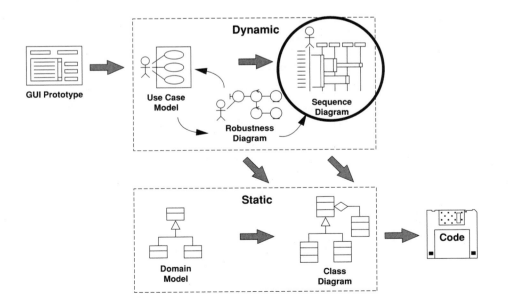

Don't be surprised if all the material in this chapter does not register with you the first time you go through it. We had been supporting Jacobson's object interaction diagram in our CASE tools for about a year before I figured out what it was all about. As I recall, it was during a conversation with an Objectory mentor (Doug Bennett, of Syrinx) that the light bulb lit for me. It's not surprising that many newcomers to the UML, and to visual modeling in general, don't pick this up immediately. The phrase *behavior allocation*, about which I go into detail later in this chapter, was the one that helped me to understand the topic.

You may think of interaction modeling as representing the changing of the guard between analysis and design. This is the point at which you take your preliminary designs from robustness analysis and drive them forward into a fully detailed object-oriented design, all the while maintaining your ability to trace the results back to your original use cases.

Jacobson provided a straightforward description of the need for interaction modeling in his business process reengineering (BPR) book:

> It is only after you have drawn interaction diagrams [called "sequence diagrams" in the UML] for all courses of events in all use cases that you can be certain that you have found all of the roles that the system requires each object to play and, thus, the responsibilities of each object.

Goals of Interaction Modeling

You want to achieve three primary goals during interaction modeling.

1. *Allocate behavior among boundary, entity, and control objects.* During robustness analysis, we identified (or at least took an educated guess at) a set of objects that together could accomplish the desired behavior of our use cases. We also broke that behavior down into discrete units and created placeholder control objects for each of those units of behavior. Now we need to decide which objects are responsible for which bits of behavior.

 If you don't have a good idea of what the relevant boundary, entity, and control objects are, it's too soon for you to be contemplating how you will allocate behavior. Go back to robustness analysis and make sure.

ALERT! ***Don't try to allocate behavior among objects before you have a good idea what the objects are.***

I recommend that you adopt a responsibility-driven thought process, along the lines of the approach first proposed by Rebecca Wirfs-Brock (*Designing Object-Oriented Software*, Prentice Hall, 1990), when you make these decisions. I'll also introduce you to some criteria, which Grady Booch defined, that should help to guide you toward good design decisions.

This is also the time to get more specific about how you will implement functionality such as error handling and business rule processing. As I discussed in the previous chapter, it's likely that many of your control objects (controllers) will turn into operations on boundary and/or entity objects during interaction modeling. (In some cases, they will stay as control objects—for example, use case controllers.)

2. *Show the detailed interactions that occur over time among the objects associated with each of your use cases.* Objects interact by sending messages to each other. These messages serve as what Jacobson calls stimuli—that is, a message stimulates an object to perform some desired action. For each unit of behavior within a use case, you must identify the necessary messages/methods.

3. *Finalize the distribution of operations among classes.* In Chapter 4, I indicated that you should aim to have a fairly high percentage (perhaps 75 or 80 percent) of your attributes defined within the static model when you finish with robustness analysis. In contrast, I advocated a minimalist approach to defining operations during domain modeling and robustness analysis. In fact, I told you not to assign *any* methods just yet. That is because there isn't enough information available with which to make good design decisions about operations at that stage of a project.

When we get to interaction modeling, however, we do have good information (at least we hope to). As you lay out the detailed behavior of your objects, on sequence diagrams, in the context of your use cases, you should begin to finalize the process of finding appropriate homes for attributes and operations. While you do this *dynamic* modeling, you will be updating and expanding your *static* model, which will solidify your increasing knowledge of how your new system should work.

The remaining sections in this chapter explain how you should go about reaching these goals.

Sequence Diagrams

The UML's **sequence diagram** evolved from Jacobson's object interaction diagram and the event trace diagram from OMT.

Within our approach, ***sequence diagrams represent the major work product of design***. You draw one sequence diagram that encompasses the basic course and *all alternative courses* within each of your use cases. (You can use more than one page if you need to.) The results form the core of your dynamic model, in which the behavior of your system at run time, including *how* the system will accomplish that behavior, is defined in great detail.

There are four types of elements on a sequence diagram.

1. *The text for the course of action of the use case* appears down the left-hand side. As you'll see in the examples that appear later in the chapter, it's a good idea to break up the text with white space so that it's easy to see which sentence corresponds with each set of elements to the right.

2. *Objects*, which you bring over directly from your robustness diagrams, are represented with two components. The name of an object and (optionally) the class to which that object belongs appear in a box at the top of the page, in the form *object::class*. A dotted line runs from that box down the length of the page. You can show the robustness diagram icons above the object boxes.

3. *Messages* are arrows between objects. A message arrow can go directly between two dotted lines, between a line and a method rectangle, or between two method rectangles (see below).

4. *Methods (operations)* are shown as rectangles that lie on top of the dotted lines that belong to the objects to which you're assigning the methods. You can use the lengths of these rectangles to reflect the *focus of control* within the sequence: a particular method is in control up to the point at which its rectangle ends.

Figure 5-1 shows samples of sequence diagram notation.

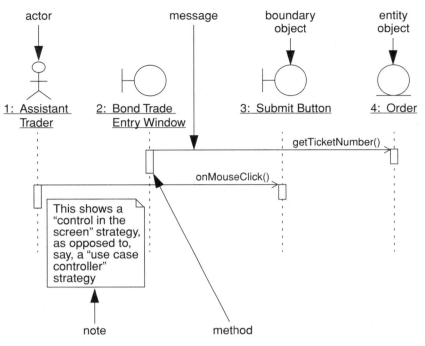

Figure 5-1 *Sequence Diagram Elements*

Getting Started

As I mentioned in the previous chapter, sequence diagrams are fairly involved and tedious to draw because they are densely packed with information. This also makes them hard to read unless we take special care to make them readable.

 However, I also told you that having proper robustness diagrams, associated with rigorously defined use cases, in place makes the job significantly easier.

ALERT! ***Don't start drawing a sequence diagram before you've completed the associated robustness diagram.***

In fact, if you're using a tool such as Rational Rose, you can "automagically" start a sequence diagram from a robustness diagram, as we'll see later in the chapter.

If I have a pet peeve about the UML, it's that it deemphasizes robustness analysis—that is, preliminary design—the result of which is that it implicitly encourages people to skip from analysis to detailed design. In that circumstance, a designer must address several types of questions at once—in the process of trying simultaneously to figure out *what* is supposed to happen from the user's standpoint, and *how* to build something in response to that. And that's where critical mistakes occur.

Separating the *what* from the *how* (see page 62) is a critical aspect of this approach, as is having a clear transition between them.

If you follow the ICONIX approach, the first three steps involved in drawing sequence diagrams are completely mechanical in nature. That can be very useful in achieving momentum as you get serious about your design.

It's been my experience that many people get stuck at this point in a development project. (This is especially likely if they've skipped preliminary design.) The technique I describe below evolved from helping students get "unstuck" during dozens of training workshops over the past five years.

Figure 5-2 shows the four steps you should perform when drawing sequence diagrams.

Follow the following three steps to start a sequence diagram.

1. *Copy the text for the given use case* from the use case specification. Paste it onto the left margin of the page.

   The project team will have put a lot of effort into writing the use case text, and the user community should have signed off on the results. Also, **the robustness models will have demonstrated feasibility in the context of the object model**—in other words, we've found some objects that we think can work together to provide the required behavior.

   At this point, then, we've done the following:

   • *Validated* the use case text with our users
   • *Double-checked* to make sure we're obeying the rules of robustness analysis
   • *Refined* the use case text so that it explicitly references objects from the domain model

Use case text is refined during robustness analysis and reviewed during the preliminary design review.

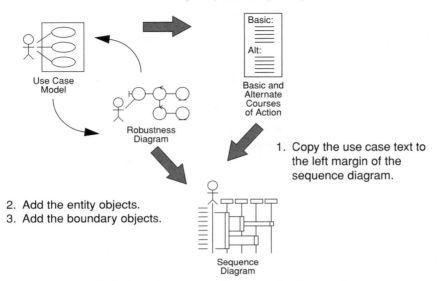

Use Case
Model

Basic and
Alternate
Courses
of Action

Robustness
Diagram

1. Copy the use case text to the left margin of the sequence diagram.

2. Add the entity objects.
3. Add the boundary objects.

Sequence
Diagram

4. Work through the controllers, one at a time, and figure out how to allocate the behavior among the collaborating objects.

The user requirements are always visible as we work through the design of the system.

Figure 5-2 *Building a Sequence Diagram*

- *Honed* our concept of the user interface
- *Reviewed* the requirements review and preliminary design

We've also made sure that we haven't violated any of the top 10 principles.

It's time, then, to take a deep breath and plunge forward into design.

We can assume that the text of each use case represents a *contractual agreement* about how the associated piece of the system will behave. Copying use case text to begin the corresponding sequence diagram enables that text to serve as an ongoing reminder of what you're trying to accomplish. The result of this is that *when you're doing the design, the required system behavior is always staring you in the face*.

Figure 5-3 shows the text for the basic course of action and the alternate course of action for the Enter Buy Trade use case, which will serve as the focus of this section.

Note that each sentence and sentence fragment has some white space around it. As you build your diagram, you should line up the message(s) associated with each piece of text as closely as possible. This will enable people reading the diagram to easily see how the system will accomplish the specified behavior.

Basic Course

The system creates a new trade with the ticket number from the order and also brings up a Bond Trade Entry window. The AT uses this window to enter the appropriate values for the associated trade.

When the AT chooses to submit the trade, the system validates both general trade values and bond-specific values (for instance, it makes sure the coupon rate is "reasonable") before processing the trade.

If the trade passes all validation tests, the system submits it to the Trade Queue, from which the trade is later sent to the Back Office System for further clearing and processing.

Alternate Course

If the validation fails, notify the user, highlight the erroneous values, and get new values from the user.

Figure 5-3 *Starting the Sequence Diagram (Step 1)*

Please keep in mind that a hard-to-read sequence diagram is, for all practical purposes, of no use. The purpose of visual modeling is to make the design visible—and *reviewable*—before any code gets written.

Note: If you do not have all the relevant alternate courses of action written out for each of your use cases, do *not* proceed with your sequence diagram until those courses are in place. The diagrams will not cover all special cases, and you will not uncover all the behavior of the use case. ***This means that you won't discover all of the necessary methods for your objects***. Check again. Go back to Chapters 3 (use cases) and 4 (robustness analysis) as necessary.

2. *Add the entity objects* from the robustness diagram.

    Each of these objects is an instance of a class that appears on the class diagram that represents your static model. (If you forgot to update your static class diagrams in response to new objects discovered during robustness analysis, ***do it now***, as I recommended at the end of Chapter 4. These objects should have most of their attributes in place. Many of them will be serving data to other objects.) You can expect to discover missing attributes as you work through your sequence diagram. Be religious about adding them to your static model; this is likely to be your last step before code.

    See Figure 5-4.

3. *Add the boundary objects* from the robustness diagram. (See Figure 5-5. Note that I'm showing these separately for space reasons.)

    You get a bonus point if you're wondering why I didn't mention adding boundary objects to your domain model. The reason is that these objects are part of the solution space; the domain model addresses the problem space. By accounting for boundary objects on your sequence diagrams, you begin integrating the two spaces at the start of detailed design.

    It's nice to keep a "clean" set of domain classes on a pure domain model diagram. However, it's also a good idea to draw "localized" static class diagrams that show *both* solution space objects and problem space objects. A good guideline for this is one such diagram per package of use cases. (Refer to Chapter 3 for a discussion of use case packages.)

1: Order   2: Trade   3: Trade Queue

BASIC COURSE:

The system creates a new
trade with the ticket number
from the order and also brings
up a Bond Trade Entry window.
The AT uses this window to
enter the appropriate values
for the associated trade.

When the AT chooses to submit
the trade, the system validates
both general trade values and
bond-specific values (for instance,
it makes sure the coupon
rate is "reasonable") before
processing the trade.

If the trade passes all validation
tests, the system submits it to the
Trade Queue, from which the trade
is later sent to the Back Office
System for clearing and further
processing.

ALTERNATE COURSE:

If the validation fails, notify the user,
highlight the erroneous values,
and get new values from the user.

Figure 5-4 *Adding Entity Objects (Step 2)*

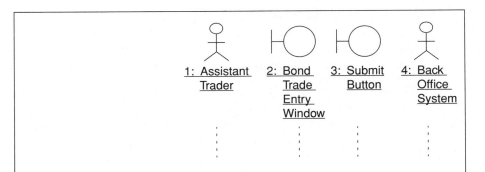

BASIC COURSE:

The system creates a new
trade with the ticket number
from the order and also brings
up a Bond Trade Entry window.
The AT uses this window to
enter the appropriate values
for the associated trade.

When the AT chooses to submit
the trade, the system validates
both general trade values and
bond-specific values (for instance,
it makes sure the coupon
rate is "reasonable") before
processing the trade.

If the trade passes all validation
tests, the system submits it to the
Trade Queue, from which the trade
is later sent to the Back Office
System for clearing and further
processing.

ALTERNATE COURSE:

If the validation fails, notify the user,
highlight the erroneous values,
and get new values from the user.

Figure 5-5 *Adding Actors and Boundary Objects (Step 3)*

We can also show actors on the left side of a sequence diagram. (In fact, because the UML doesn't contain Jacobson's "system boundary" symbol, it's often necessary to do this.) So, from left to right, we have use case text, actors, boundary objects, and entity objects.

Note that these three steps are easy to automate. If you have good robustness diagrams that you created with a visual modeling tool such as Rose, you can write scripts to tell the tool to generate skeleton sequence diagrams. That saves you time for the next step. Having your tool put the use case text, actors, entity objects, and boundary objects in place will save you effort and ensure precision, as well, as you will be able to select your objects in the order in which you want them to appear on your diagrams.

The following is a script from my Rose 98 tutorial CD-ROM that you can use in Rose to generate a sequence diagram from a robustness diagram. Just select your actors, boundary objects, and entity objects in the order in which you want them to appear on your sequence diagram, and run it!

```
Sub Main
    Dim theModel As Model
    Dim thePackage As Category
    Dim myDiagram As ScenarioDiagram
    Dim anObject As ObjectInstance
    Dim theClasses As ClassCollection
    Dim theAssoc As Association
    Dim theAssociations As AssociationCollection
    Dim theRole As Role
    Dim aClass As Class

    Viewport.Open

    Set theModel = RoseApp.CurrentModel
    Set thePackage = theModel.RootUseCaseCategory
    Set theClasses = theModel.getSelectedClasses
    Set myDiagram = thePackage.AddScenarioDiagram
        ("newSequenceDiagram",1)
    Print "Creating sequence diagram with the
        following objects:"
    Set theClasses = theModel.GetSelectedClasses
```

```
    For i = 1 To theClasses.Count
        Print theClasses.GetAt(i).name
        Set aClass = theClasses.GetAt(i)
        result = myDiagram.AddInstance
            ("object",aClass.name)
    Next i

    myDiagram.Layout
End Sub
```

Once you're done with these steps, you're over the hump of getting your design started, and it's time to move on to the real work.

Putting Methods on Classes

Deciding which methods go on which classes is the essence of interaction modeling.

Unfortunately, it's also pretty hard, compared with the relatively easy tasks we've talked about so far in this book. That's because you really have to think through every decision, large or small. Experience and talent are required here. This is why I advised you, in Chapter 3, to make use of mechanisms for factoring out commonality (such as invokes). Repeating the same hard work many times in-line on your sequence diagrams is counterproductive.

However, there is a bright side. The more experience you gain in object-oriented design (OOD), the easier it becomes to make good decisions. Also, there are often several reasonably good ways to allocate behavior across a group of objects.

I like to present a riddle in my training classes to help my students understand the thought process involved in allocating behavior among objects. We have a cow that needs milking. The question is: Does the *Cow* object milk itself, or does the *Milk* object "de-cow" itself? (The correct answer, naturally, is that the *Milking Machine* actor invokes the Dispense Milk method on the *Udder* boundary object!)

So, where do we start? As you may have guessed, we can get a head start by working from our robustness diagrams.

The fourth step in doing a sequence diagram, putting methods on classes, involves *converting the controllers* from your robustness diagram, one at a time, to sets of methods and messages that embody the desired behavior. (Occasionally, you might elect to turn a controller into a real control object. I address this strategy in the second example later in this chapter.)

Along these lines, I suggest that you *use your robustness diagram as a checklist* to make sure you have all the required system behavior accounted for on your sequence diagrams. You simply check off each control object as you draw the corresponding message(s) on the sequence diagrams. This will help you eliminate the "oops, I forgot about that function" error—which, as you might guess, is an insidious one. (Note that one controller on a robustness diagram can translate to several methods on a sequence diagram.)

You've already checked the robustness diagrams against your use case text. By checking your sequence diagrams against your robustness diagrams, you add a measure of assurance that *you're designing in response to what the user needs* (in other words, meeting your requirements).

This step in the ICONIX approach represents your entry into what we might think of as the second half of the fundamental object-oriented development theme. In the first half, you focused on identifying the objects. Now, you will figure out how to assign behavior to those objects.

You must answer two big questions.

1.   What are the objects?
2.   Which objects are *responsible for* which functions?

Question 2 has its foundation in Rebecca Wirfs-Brock's Responsibility-Driven Design. Dan Rawsthorne, formerly one of my instructors at ICONIX, offers a great way to summarize the responsibility-driven philosophy: An object (and, by extension, a class) should have a single "personality," and we should do our best to avoid "schizophrenic" objects. This means that a class should be focused on a strongly related set of behaviors.

So if you have an object with a split personality—or multiple personalities—you should use aggregation, which I discussed in Chapter 2, to split it up. As I mentioned there, *discordant* attributes—attributes that don't seem to fit in with their peers—are usually indicative of a schizophrenic object.

Many people find Class-Responsibility-Collaboration (CRC) cards useful in addressing behavior allocation. The Wirfs-Brock book is a good starting point for learning about CRC cards. Figure 5-6 shows what one looks like.

Behavior allocation—deciding which operations belong to which classes—is of *critical* importance in the approach I describe in this book. Decisions made during this phase of a project dictate whether the overall design is good or bad. This is where experienced designers earn their pay.

Our approach identifies behavior in use case analysis, nails the behavior down and "quantizes" it during robustness analysis, and allocates that behavior to objects on the sequence diagrams.

In Chapter 4, you learned that your control objects (controllers) serve as placeholders for the desired functionality of the new system. If you do a thorough job of robustness analysis, you call out all the important processing steps that need to occur in order for the system to carry out the use case for which you're doing detailed design.

☰□	Class Card	□☰
Class: Ambient Light Sensor	☐ **Abstract** ☒ **Concrete**	
Superclasses:		
Subclasses:		
Responsibility	**Collaboration**	
Turn lights on in low ambient light	Headlights	

Figure 5-6 *CRC Card*

Drawing messages between objects is equivalent to assigning methods/operations to the objects to which the message arrows point. (In Rose, they are actually one and the same step. In fact, this is one of my favorite features of Rose.)

While we're talking about messages, I suggest that you keep your diagrams free of clutter. In particular, I recommend that you don't show message parameters on your sequence diagrams.

While you are making behavior allocation decisions, you are making decisions that affect the quality of the classes in your design. I learned about the following criteria from Grady Booch's *Object-Oriented Analysis and Design with Applications* (Addison-Wesley, 1994).

I keep these criteria in mind at all times when I'm deciding which methods belong with which objects on my sequence diagrams.

- *Reusability.* The more general your objects and classes, the higher the probability that you'll be able to reuse those objects and classes for other projects. Ask yourself whether assigning a method to a class makes that class more or less reusable.

- *Applicability.* The concept of applicability is basically the same in the context of interaction modeling as it is for domain modeling and use case modeling. When you assign methods to the objects on your sequence diagrams, always ask yourself whether there seems to be a good fit between method and object, and also whether the task the method performs is obviously relevant to the object.

- *Complexity.* Our first two criteria, reusability and applicability, are still somewhat theoretical. The subject of complexity is an indication that we're about to get serious about implementation issues. In essence, the issue here is whether it's easier to build a method in one or another object.

- *Implementation Knowledge.* This criterion involves asking whether the implementation of the behavior depends on details internal to the associated method.

Examples

Figure 5-7 shows the sequence diagram we started building in the "Getting Started" section of this chapter for the Enter Buy Trade use case.

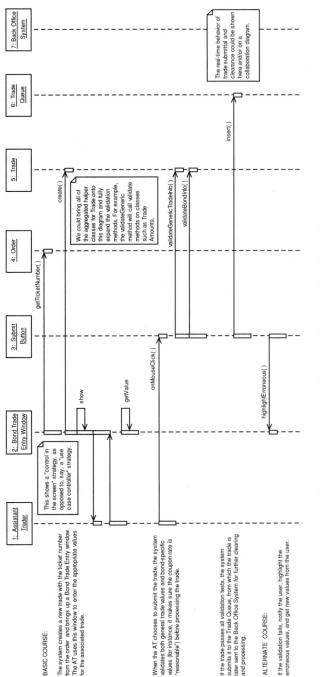

Figure 5-7 *Sequence Diagram for Enter Buy Trade Use Case*

Before we examine the use case text, look at the note that sits under the first two objects from the left. This sequence diagram reflects a design strategy that involves putting various aspects of the control logic on the boundary objects. The example that appears later in this section involves leaving most of that logic within a control object. I'm not going to recommend one strategy over the other here; these are two possible strategies (out of many) that you can follow to good effect.

The beginning of the first sentence of the use case text implicitly refers to the Perform Order Entry use case, which precedes Enter Buy Trade (see Figure 3-8). This is why the first two messages to other objects (getTicketNumber and create) come from the *Bond Trade Entry* window, even though the *Assistant Trader* (AT) actor is the first element in the body of the sequence diagram. The latter part of the first sentence forms the true beginning of this use case from the AT's standpoint.

When the AT presses the Submit pushbutton on the *Bond Trade Entry* window, the system will call two "validate" methods. As indicated by the note above the validateGenericTradeInfo message, I've deferred showing full detail about which validation occurs on which helper class. Supplementary sequence diagrams would show, for instance, a validateDates method on the *Trade* class that checks to see that the repayment start date precedes the repayment end date.

The third note on the diagram says that I could show more detail here or on a collaboration diagram. In fact, I decided to use a collaboration diagram in the next chapter (see Figure 6-1).

Wherever possible, you should try to fit the alternative course(s) of your use case on the same sequence diagram with the basic course. In this case, the alternative course is straightforward and requires no further comment.

I mentioned earlier that you might choose to leave your robustness diagram controllers as control objects on your sequence diagram (and, thus, detailed design). Figure 5-8 shows the beginnings of a sequence diagram for the Perform Order Entry use case that uses this approach.

Note that there's not as much white space between the sentences of the use case text as there was on the previous sequence diagram. This is because, as you can see, this diagram is an unfinished piece of work. We'd normally be adding more space between the sentences as we create the associated messages.

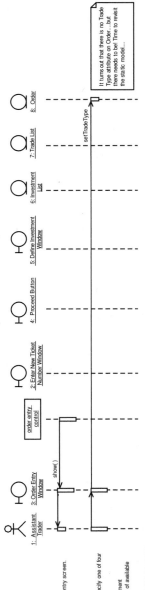

Figure 5-8 *Sequence Diagram for Perform Order Entry Use Case*

As we begin to walk through Perform Order Entry, our order entry control object has control. So the Order Entry window receives a show message rather than sending that message to itself as the Bond Trade Entry window did in Figure 5-7.

We can tie the second sentence back to the option buttons that appeared in Figure 3-3. Once the AT clicks one of those buttons, the system will try to establish the corresponding value within an *Order* object. However, there's a problem: *Order* doesn't have an appropriate attribute.

As I've shown in the note next to *Order*, this calls for a visit to the static model so that we can create a tradeType attribute. Note, though, that we should have foreseen this on the robustness diagram for this use case (see Figure 4-5), when we forgot to connect the SpecifyTradeType controller to the *Order* object.

Do we have to go back? Maybe not. The robustness diagram served its purpose by getting us started, and remember: Robustness diagrams, unlike sequence diagrams, are meant to be disposable. This does, however, illustrate the importance of reviewing your robustness models carefully.

The latter example is typical of what you have to go through to get your sequence diagrams, and thus your detailed design, right. At each step of the process, we fix errors we made during the previous step. This is normal. (Don't feel badly when it happens—it's much better to do that than to fix errors during beta testing of the released system.) I warned you that it wasn't going to be easy!

As you can see from these examples, designing classes and drawing sequence diagrams is real work, no question about it. However, if you keep in mind the principles I just discussed, and you approach the task in the same incremental and iterative manner that I've suggested throughout this book, you'll have an excellent chance to get it right. Please remember, however, that there is no single right answer; there are many ways to create a design and end up with working code.

Updating Your Static Model

As you should be well aware by now, you need to continue to refine your static model, as shown in Figure 5-9.

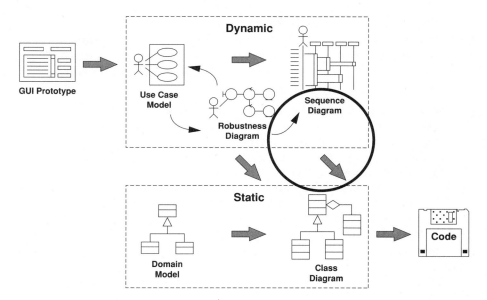

Figure 5-9 *Updating Your Static Model, Again*

The following sections will guide you in the refinement process up to the point at which you're ready to start coding.

Finalizing Attributes and Methods

To start, add attributes and methods to your classes as soon as you decide where they go in the context of your sequence diagrams. In some tools, including Rational Rose, you can add an operation to a class directly on a sequence diagram, by right-clicking on the message arrow. I'd say that captures the essence of driving the static model from the dynamic model!

 Note, however, that you should *not* spend lots of time adding get and set methods to your model. You should take advantage of the principle of encapsulation: Only allow access to attributes via "getters" and "setters." But, you can readily generate get and set methods for each relevant class by using a script such as the one I talk about next.

ALERT! *Don't focus on get and set methods instead of focusing on real methods.*

The following excerpts are from a script that loops through the classes you select, including all attributes and associations, and creates the get and set methods that each class will need, if they don't already exist. It was written by Robert Zembowicz (see **http://www.robertz.com**).

```
Sub GenerateGetSetForAttributes(class As Class)
    Dim attributes As AttributeCollection
    Dim attribute As Attribute
    'loop through all attributes
    Set attributes = class.Attributes
    For attrID = 1 To attributes.Count
        Set attribute = attributes.GetAt(attrID)
        GenerateGetSetOperations class, attribute.Name,
          attribute.Type, "attribute"
    Next attrID
End Sub
Function GetRoleName(association As Association, role As
  Role) As String
    If role.Navigable Then
      If role.Name <> "" Then
          GetRoleName = role.Name
      Else
          GetRoleName = association.Name
      End If
    Else
      GetRoleName = ""
    End If
End Function
```

Ensuring Quality

Now is a good time to think about your classes and ask yourself if they satisfy the following quality criteria.

- **Coupling** is a measure of the strength of a connection between two classes. You can improve the modularity of a system by designing it with *loose coupling* wherever possible. This translates into classes that are highly independent.

- **Cohesion** is a measure of how tightly connected the attributes and operations of a class are. It is desirable to strive for *high functional cohesion*, which occurs when the elements of each of your classes are all working together to provide a clearly defined behavior (in other words, a single personality).

- **Sufficiency** is the condition in which a class encapsulates enough of the abstractions your models present so that it offers something meaningful and efficient, with which other parts of the system can interact. The key question is whether the class covers all the relevant cases.

- **Completeness** is the condition in which a given class's interface captures all the relevant abstractions. So a complete class is one that is theoretically reusable in any number of contexts. Keep in mind, though, that it's not often a good idea to overdo your efforts in this direction—you might never get anything built.

- **Primitiveness** is the condition in which an operation can be efficiently built only if it has access to the material on which your models are built. The idea here is that you can design certain operations that you can use as building blocks for other operations as your design evolves.

Adding Infrastructure

As you come up with scaffolding and other types of infrastructure, such as "helper" classes, put them on the static class diagram, as well. This is where you shift your focus from the problem space to the solution space. It's best to use localized class diagrams—say, one per use case package—because, by this time, your static model is probably too expansive to be captured within one readable diagram. Doing this also allows work to be split across teams.

The static model should evolve continuously, from the initial "architect's rendering" of the domain model through to the point at which it becomes the "software blueprint" from which you'll code the new system. This evolutionary process is *driven by the use cases* through the sequence diagrams, and even beyond.

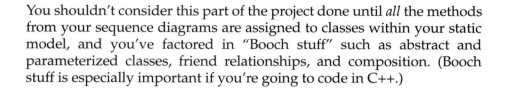

You shouldn't consider this part of the project done until *all* the methods from your sequence diagrams are assigned to classes within your static model, and you've factored in "Booch stuff" such as abstract and parameterized classes, friend relationships, and composition. (Booch stuff is especially important if you're going to code in C++.)

Patternizing Your Design

Earlier in the chapter, I discussed two strategies for converting controllers that appear on robustness diagrams: "control in the screen" and "use case controller." If you were to head in one or the other direction during your sequence diagramming efforts, that would qualify as patternizing.

The idea is that the team members who are responsible for the diagrams should establish, early in this task, some design standards that can be used across all your use cases.

Looking in another direction: As you're diagramming the interactions among the various objects, you may decide that one or more well-established design patterns would fit in nicely.

You might choose to use the *Factory Method* pattern, which lets a class defer instantiation to subclasses, or *Iterator*, which lets a client traverse a list in various ways, without needing to know how that list has been implemented. (See Gamma, Helm, Johnson, and Vlissides, *Design Patterns*, Addison-Wesley, 1995.) Or perhaps you might develop new patterns in order to establish a standardized approach to design problems that appear across multiple use cases.

This is the time to make these kinds of decisions—domain modeling is *not* the time!

Back to the Example

Figure 5-10 shows excerpts of the updated static model for our example system, with attributes suppressed on the display.

We're not going to try to repeat all the good stuff from *Design Patterns* or the Booch book here; note that this is the time in your project at which you can benefit from the strategies presented in those books.

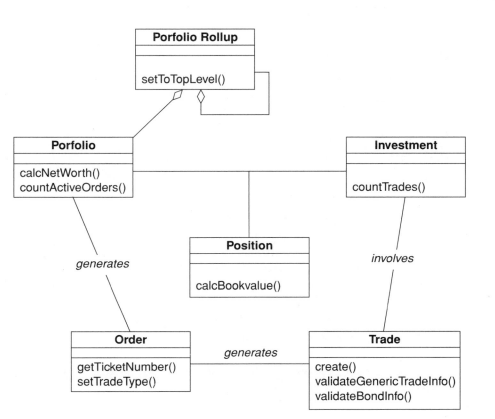

Figure 5-10 *Design-Level Class Diagram*

Completing Interaction Modeling

You're finished with interaction modeling when you've drawn all the necessary sequence diagrams and updated your static model in turn (see Figure 5-11).

This is likely to be your last stop before code, so please note that critical design review (CDR) is *essential* before you go on. I'll also remind you of the critical importance of OO experience as you proceed.

If you're building a real-time embedded system, or if you discern the need for a deeper exploration of the ways your objects work together,

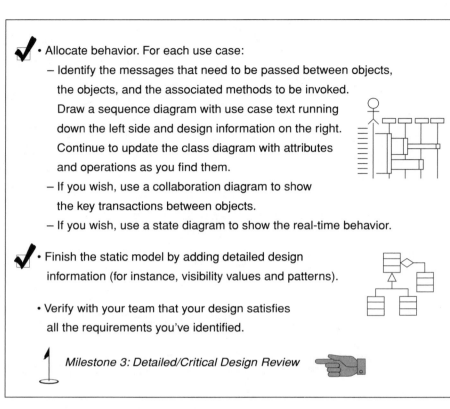

Figure 5-11 *Design Checkpoint 1*

proceed to the next chapter. Otherwise, skip to Chapter 7 to learn more about how you should be able to trace every piece of work you do as part of the Unified Object Modeling approach back to user requirements.

Top 10 Points to Remember
When Drawing Sequence Diagrams

10. *You need to do one sequence diagram for each use case.*

9. *The diagram should match the narrative flow of the associated use case.*

8. *Whenever possible, do a single sequence diagram for the entire use case, including all alternative courses of action. Split the diagram only when a single diagram for the use case gets too difficult to manage.*

7. *Messages between objects invoke the operations on the classes.*

6. *If you're having trouble getting a sequence diagram started, you probably wrote the use case incorrectly and/or didn't complete robustness analysis.*

5. *By exploring the dynamic behavior of the system, you learn which attributes and operations are needed in the classes contained within your static model.*

4. *Remember that the sequence diagram is the primary vehicle for making behavior allocation decisions. You're really using your sequence diagrams to assign operations to your classes as you go.*

3. *You are adding solution space objects to the problem domain objects as you explore system usage at a detailed level. Solution space objects include boundary (interface) objects from the robustness diagrams.*

2. *You incorporate infrastructure, scaffolding, and helper objects into your designs at this point. Design patterns are often helpful here; this is where much of real OOD takes place.*

1. *Writing the original requirements-level text for the use case in the margin of the sequence diagram provides visual requirements traceability from the design back to your user-certified requirements.*

Chapter 6

Collaboration and State Modeling

You can use the UML's collaboration diagram and state diagram in conjunction with your sequence diagrams to model additional aspects of the dynamic behavior of the system you are designing. Typically, collaboration diagrams and state diagrams are most useful in the design of real-time systems, or when you need to explain the real-time aspects of client/server or other distributed systems.

Collaboration diagrams are closely related to sequence diagrams and are logically part of interaction modeling. In fact, it's relatively easy to

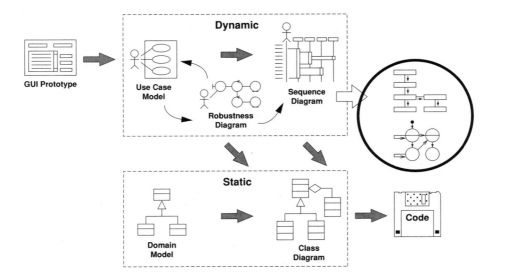

generate collaboration diagrams from sequence diagrams, and vice versa. I pair them with state diagrams because within the ICONIX Unified Object Modeling approach, they're both optional. You should use either or both when they add value above and beyond your sequence diagrams (of which you should have at least one for each of your use cases).

 Before you go further in this chapter, you should know that the other reason I've grouped these together is because I've found that excessive use of these diagrams can be a leading cause of analysis paralysis. It's very easy, for instance, to fall into the trap of cranking out lots of state diagrams for objects with two potential states, like Cancel and OK. If, however, you have a genuine need to capture complex object behavior, then collaboration diagrams and state diagrams can be useful.

ALERT! *Don't do state diagrams for objects with two states.*

Remember: The UML is an inclusive superset of almost everything that was in Booch's, Rumbaugh's, and Jacobson's original methodologies. The subject of state diagrams is one area in which there tends to be a significant difference between theory and practice with regard to the utility and cost-effectiveness of building models. Just as you don't need to use every word that appears in the dictionary, *you don't need to use every element of the UML.*

When Do We Need Collaboration Diagrams?

A **collaboration diagram** shows how objects associated with a use case *collaborate* to perform critical pieces of the behavior the use case calls for. This type of diagram evolved directly (read: was renamed) from Booch's object diagram. (Note that the UML object diagram is different.)

Although collaboration diagrams and sequence diagrams both show detailed interactions among objects, in the form of message passing, a collaboration diagram focuses the view on only the *key transactions* within a scenario—in other words, the collaboration diagram emphasizes organization—while sequence diagrams follow the narrative flow of entire use cases—the emphasis is on the time ordering. I prefer the sequence diagram because it is *traceable* to the use case.

Within this focused view of the collaboration diagram, we can see additional details. Specifically, ***collaboration diagrams add extra detail related to the timing of the messages***. (Although it's possible to show this detail on a sequence diagram, I usually don't.)

This means that collaboration diagrams should come into play when you need to show additional detail about timing for the key transactions within your scenario. The corollary is that ***we usually don't need them the rest of the time***.

I generally choose a sequence diagram over a collaboration diagram because of the former's traceability and coverage of an entire scenario. You probably don't have time to do redundant modeling of object interactions on both sequence diagrams and collaboration diagrams. Here again, the fact that the UML provides multiple ways to say the same thing is probably not an advantage. If you have a strong preference for collaboration diagrams, though, use them. Just make sure you account for all the required behavior in your design.

Grady Booch has defined four standard types of messages.

1. A *synchronous* message corresponds with a method within a receiving object starting to execute only when the sending object has sent a message and the receiver is ready to accept that message.

2. A *balking* message is equivalent to a synchronous message, except the sending object gives up on the message if the receiving object is not ready to accept it.

3. A *timeout* message is equivalent to a synchronous message, except the sending object waits only for a specified period for the receiving object to get ready to accept the message.

4. An *asynchronous* message involves the sending object being able to send the message regardless of whether the receiving object is ready to accept it.

As on a sequence diagram, objects appear on a collaboration diagram as rectangles, and messages are shown as arrows. On a collaboration diagram, however, you can indicate the sequence of messages with numbers.

Figure 6-1 shows a collaboration diagram that illustrates how we might clear and book a trade within our example system.

There are three ways to address message numbering.

1. You can use integers to show only the basic sequence. Consecutive numbers indicate a specific order of message passing; you can also use duplicate numbers to show messages that can be sent in parallel.

2. You can use decimal numbers to show which objects invoke which other objects. For instance, if one object calls another object (by sending a message), which turns around and calls a third object, you might number the associated messages 1, 1.1, and 1.1.1, respectively.

3. You can skip numbering altogether, as I do.

The UML standard is decimal numbering, but some think decimals tend to make it harder to see the overall flow of the collaboration. You should use whatever style of numbering works best for you.

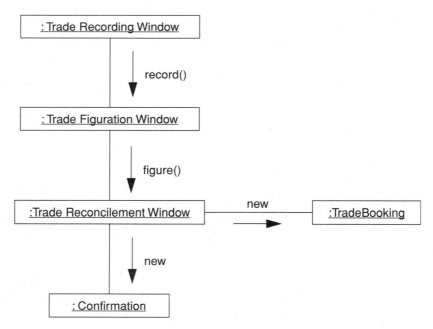

Figure 6-1 *Collaboration Diagram*

State Diagrams

A **state diagram** captures the lifecycle of one or more objects. This cycle is expressed in terms of the different states that the objects can assume and the events that cause changes in state.

Events can come from external sources, such as other objects (for example, a message), a clock (the passing of a specified period of time), or internal sources (such as a condition becoming true).

The basic elements of state diagrams are:

- The initial state (such as the creation of an object) appears as a solid black circle. If you want to show final states (including object destruction), you draw a solid black circle inside a larger, hollow circle.

- Each state is represented in a rectangle that has rounded corners. This rectangle must contain at least the name of the state. If you are defining activities that will take place in the context of a state, you split the rectangle, as you would in a class diagram.

  The UML offers three standard types of events that correspond with activities:

  1. *Entry*—Perform the associated activity as soon as the object reaches this state.
  2. *Exit*—Perform the activity as the object is leaving this state.
  3. *Do*—Perform the activity at the appropriate point while the object is in this state.

- A transition is shown as an arrow between two states. You can name the event associated with a transition. You can also assign a **guard**, which is simply a logical condition that can be either True or False; the associated transition will occur only on a True.

A sample state diagram appears later in this chapter.

How Many State Diagrams Do We Need?

As with collaboration diagrams, a key question regarding state diagrams relates to how many of them a project really needs. OO theory tells us that each object in a system has its own **state machine**, which describes how the object is instantiated (created), how it sends messages to and receives messages from other objects, and how it is destroyed at the end of its useful life. While this is true, the reality is that many objects have boring state machines, and time spent diagramming these is not productive time.

 Understanding what needs to be modeled—and what can be avoided—is one of the most important aspects of avoiding analysis paralysis.

ALERT! *Don't model what you don't really need to model.*

As far as state machines go, I prefer, in many cases, to see state diagrams (if necessary) at the use case level rather than at the individual object level. (I don't want to think about the number of projects to which I've been exposed in which people spent time drawing state diagrams for objects with two states: On and Off. I call these light-switch objects, which makes my point clearly.)

As you look at your robustness diagrams, the number of control objects should give you a clue to how much state modeling might be appropriate. As a rule of thumb, I look for between two and five controllers for a use case.

 If you have a use case with five or six controllers sending messages back and forth, it's likely that a state diagram or two might clarify things somewhat. If you have, say, 10 controllers, the odds are even better, especially if you have controllers talking to other controllers. However, if your use case is not very control-intensive, it's probably just as well not to bother; "state-machine-itis" is a leading cause of analysis paralysis on OO projects.

ALERT! *Don't do state diagrams just because you can.*

Figure 6-2 is a state diagram that shows the substates associated with a *Trade* object within our sample system.

The UML allows you to build hierarchies of state diagrams. This is fine in theory, and it may actually have practical application in such areas as avionics. However, in most cases, I strongly suggest that you avoid the temptation to nest several state diagrams on one (perhaps oversized) piece of paper. Instead, stick to drawing one state diagram per page, using child diagrams to show substates, as needed.

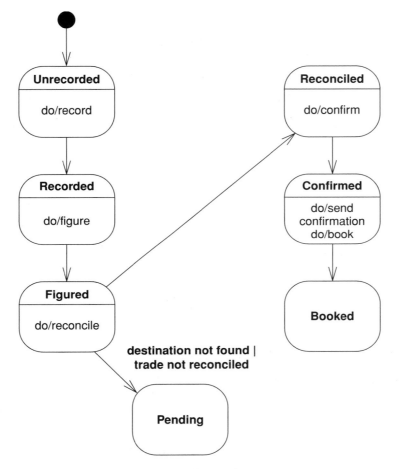

Figure 6-2 *State Diagram*

Just because you *can* do something according to UML standards doesn't mean you *should*. ***Readability is important!*** Most people, including me, have to work to understand even a single-level state diagram of moderate complexity. Why complicate life by putting multiple levels of substates on a page?

Bruce Powel Douglass' *Real-Time UML: Developing Efficient Objects for Embedded Systems* (Addison Wesley Longman, 1998) is an excellent resource about state diagrams, if you need them. The book also presents an opposing view about the utility of multi-level state diagrams, so you should definitely look into it if you feel the need to go in that direction.

Remember, real-time embedded systems are different, and you will get substantially more leverage from this area of OO theory than you will with a non-real-time system. But even if you're building a real-time system, you still need to account for all the behavior in your design, so the advice I provide in the rest of the book remains valid.

Activity Diagrams

The UML **activity diagram** captures actions and the results of those actions. (You might say that *activity diagram* is UML-speak for *flow-chart*. Actually, that's what the *UML User Guide* says, too.)

One interesting feature of this diagram is **swimlanes**, which enable you to group activities by who's performing them—for instance, the Marketing department versus Manufacturing. You might use activity diagrams when you want to explore the inner workings of operations.

Formally, the activity diagram is a degenerate form of the state diagram on which all the transitions are basically sequential. To me, however, the activity diagram (that is, flowchart) is a weak sister to the data flow diagram (DFD), which has basically been "banned in Boston" since OMT was subsumed by UML. As a result, I don't use activity diagrams. I find that regular state diagrams work better for real-time OOD, and data flow diagrams work better for showing how data flows among elements of a system.

While we're on the subject of data flow diagrams, I'd like to make a point about what seems to be a never-ending debate.

I've found OO methods to be superior, *almost* all the time, to structured analysis and the like since the key object methods appeared in the early '90s. But I do not think you should trash a technique that's known to work well in certain situations just because it's not considered "inherently" object-oriented. There's no reason why OO methods and functional methods can't be used together, as appropriate.

One example leaps to mind. While working with a client in the defense industry, I came across a need for an object called a sonar signature. Our object-oriented analysis was moving right along until we decided that sonar signatures needed to compute themselves. We were then faced with 100,000 lines of code (purely algorithmic) about how to compute this signature.

I didn't hesitate to recommend a functional decomposition for this "method," in the context of the overall OO architecture. That was the right choice in that situation—we needed to decompose one really big function into its subfunctions, rather than try to mold some OO technique to do the job. Yes, this book is about an object-oriented process for software development, but keep your mind open to all the tools and techniques that are available to you.

This is *not* to say, however, that functional decomposition is equivalent to use case analysis, which a number of otherwise well-spoken people seem to think. These people tend to draw the conclusion that the UML's extends mechanism enables functional decomposition of use cases. (Curiously, these are often the same people who are fierce advocates of the extends construct and who equate use cases with functions and thus use case modeling with functional decomposition. I have more to say about this in Chapter 7 and the appendix.) This argument is fueled by the fact that a use case diagram does look somewhat like a data flow diagram (DFD); some people do try to draw DFDs using use case notation. (As they say, good FORTRAN programmers can write FORTRAN in any language.)

I respond that if we write a user manual for a system built using object-oriented techniques, and that manual describes how a user interacts with the system's functionality, does that mean that the user manual—which, after all, reflects the use case model—represents a functional (design) decomposition? I think not. As we'll see in the next chapter, users care about having their requirements met, and the point of a use case driven approach is to ensure that they do have their requirements met. Remember: Use cases are about *building the right system*; sequence diagrams are about *building the system right*.

Extending Interaction Modeling

Figure 6-3 shows how collaboration diagrams and state diagrams fit with the principles of behavior allocation I talked about in Chapter 5.

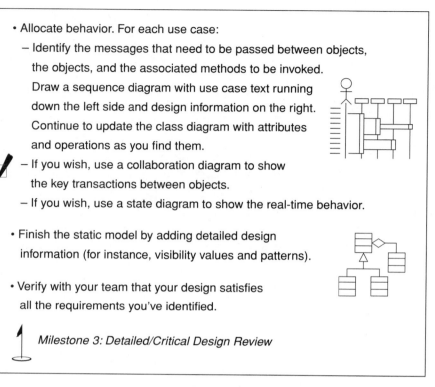

- Allocate behavior. For each use case:
  - Identify the messages that need to be passed between objects, the objects, and the associated methods to be invoked. Draw a sequence diagram with use case text running down the left side and design information on the right. Continue to update the class diagram with attributes and operations as you find them.
  - If you wish, use a collaboration diagram to show the key transactions between objects.
  - If you wish, use a state diagram to show the real-time behavior.

- Finish the static model by adding detailed design information (for instance, visibility values and patterns).

- Verify with your team that your design satisfies all the requirements you've identified.

  Milestone 3: Detailed/Critical Design Review

Figure 6-3 *Design Checkpoint 2*

Top 10 Ways to Catch a Case of Analysis Paralysis

10. *Put cardinality indicators on each end of every association on your static model.*

9. *Write one use case for every functional requirement.*

8. *Do a collaboration diagram to go with each sequence diagram, because collaboration diagrams are part of the UML.*

7. *Cover the entire scenario in every one of your collaboration diagrams. Don't focus on the key transactions.*

6. *Draw state diagrams for every class in your static model.*

5. *Spend hours fiddling with the message numbers on your collaboration diagrams.*

4. *Draw one huge multilevel hierarchical state diagram for the entire system. Show at least five levels of substates.*

3. *Jump directly from requirements-level use case views into detailed design with sequence diagrams. Do not pass go; do not collect $200; do not bother with preliminary design. (Do not call me to ask why you're stuck.)*

2. *Do lots of detailed design work before the requirements model is finished, then rework the design a bunch of times as you're finishing requirements. Even better, write a lot of code before finishing the requirements model.*

1. *Create hundreds of state diagrams, each containing two states.*

Chapter 7

Addressing Requirements

You may be wondering why I've deferred discussion of requirements to the next-to-last chapter of this book.

There are two reasons.

1. There seems to be a lot of confusion about the differences among requirements, use cases, and functions (operations). Since I talked about use cases in Chapter 3 and functions in Chapter 5, it's easier to talk about requirements in terms of how they contrast with those items.

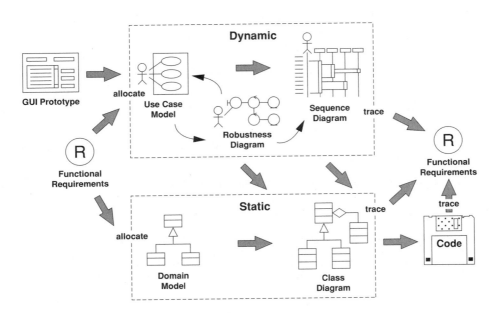

2. The concept of **traceability** becomes critical at this point in the life-cycle, when developers are getting anxious to start cutting code. I'll show you how to trace the results of your analysis and design work back to user requirements in hopes that you'll avoid implementing a system that doesn't do what your paying customers need it to do. It's hard to overemphasize the importance of this point.

It seems there are as many ways of addressing requirements as there are software development projects. I believe that if you take the ideas in this chapter to heart, you'll find your customers will be more satisfied with what you deliver.

What Is a Requirement?

Simply stated, a **requirement** is a user-specified criterion that a system must satisfy. Taken together, the requirements associated with a proposed system define the behavior and functionality required by the users of that system.

Requirements are usually expressed as sentences that include the word *shall* or the word *must*. There are many different types of requirements, including:

- *Functional* requirements ("The system shall automatically generate appropriate postings to the General Ledger.")
- *Data* requirements ("Traders must be able to execute trades involving instruments denominated in a variety of foreign currencies.")
- *Performance* requirements ("The system must validate the data that is being entered for a new trade and respond to the user within three seconds.")
- *Capacity* requirements ("The system shall be able to maintain information for up to 10,000 trades at a time.")
- *Test* requirements ("Stress testing shall involve no fewer than 50 users entering trades at one time.")

I like to treat requirements as entities that have names just as use cases and classes have. In other words, *requirements are first-class citizens* within the modeling process. This way, we avoid getting our terms mixed up and end up saying things like "use cases are requirements."

For instance, I keep pointers (name references) from each use case to each requirement satisfied by that use case, and from each class to each requirement satisfied by that class. Within that scheme, requirements can also reference lists of test cases, bug reports, and change requests, which appear during implementation and maintenance.

This approach also lends itself to automation, because software is generally better at keeping track of pointers than humans are, and it can also do useful things such as generate cross-references. I talk more about this later in the chapter.

If you're interested in requirements, I recommend you look into *The Olduvai Imperative* by Peter DeGrace and Leslie Hulet Stahl (Prentice Hall, 1993). The chapter "An Odyssey Through the Ilities," which talks about such subjects as reliability and maintainability, is one of the best treatments of this topic that I've seen.

The Nature of Requirements, Use Cases, and Functions

My view of requirements is rather different from that of some currently popular schools of thought. In particular, one author advocates building one use case for each functional requirement, which strikes me as a deeply flawed approach. Here's the way I see it.

- A use case describes a unit of behavior.
- Requirements describe the laws that govern that behavior.
- Functions are the individual actions that occur within that behavior.

You will certainly have user requirements in mind when you write your use cases, but there's no reason why a use case can't address more than one requirement. It's also perfectly acceptable to have a situation in which a combination of use cases satisfies only one requirement.

Chapter 5 talked about how you evolve your functionality and capture it in sequence diagrams from the results of robustness analysis. *Functions are the vehicle you use to answer the questions posed to your project team by the requirements.*

Let's consider an example. We have a cowboy named Billy Bob, who is driving down the road at 80 miles an hour while drinking beer, scratching, and tossing the empty beer cans out the window of his pickup truck.

Figure 7-1 is a use case diagram that shows the use cases we can identify from that last sentence, as well as the declarations we can make about how these use cases are related.

As you'll see, we're *not* employing anything resembling functional decomposition.

Here's a possible basic course of action for Drink Beer:

> Billy Bob removes one hand from the steering wheel and grabs a can of beer from the six-pack on the seat next to him. He pops the top on the can and drains it in one prolonged gulp, without removing his eyes from the road. Sometimes, Billy scratches with his other hand while he's drinking.

Writing the usage description helps us identify some objects, as shown in Figure 7-2. The behavior of the system will be distributed across these objects.

The requirements—in this case, the laws that should govern Billy Bob's behavior, in the event he's stopped by a cop—are:

1. Driving under the influence of alcohol is illegal.
2. Littering is illegal.

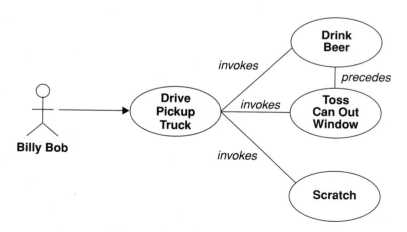

Figure 7-1 *Billy Bob's Behavior*

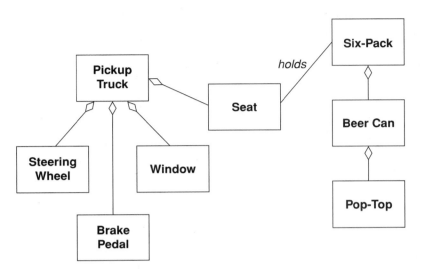

Figure 7-2 *Objects Associated with Billy Bob*

3. The speed limit of the road on which Billy Bob is driving is 65 miles per hour.

4. Billy Bob shall not toss any beer cans out the window while he is being followed by a police officer. (This is an example of a *derived* requirement. It's derived from requirement 2.)

5. Billy Bob shall slow the pickup to 65 mph while he is being followed by a police officer. (This is derived from requirement 3.)

We can define five functions based on the use cases and requirements just identified:

1. Drain Can in One Big Gulp

2. Steer Truck

3. Scratch

4. Slow Truck to 65

5. Toss Can

It should be fairly obvious how these relate to the use cases and requirements. These units of behavior are on a lower level than the ones our cowboy friend was thinking of in the first place. Even though he might do some of these activities "automatically," without thinking, these smaller units of behavior comprise the functionality of the use cases. Therefore, we'd represent them as controllers on our robustness diagrams.

Note that these functions *can* (sometimes) usefully be decomposed. For instance, Toss Can can be decomposed into Pick Up Can, Lower Window, and Toss.

The following is a basic process specification for Drink Beer:

```
Inputs
    can of beer
Outputs
    empty beer can
Function: consume can of beer
BEGIN
    Retrieve can from 6-pack
    Open can
    REPEAT
      Swallow beer
    UNTIL no more beer in can
END
```

This "mini-spec" explains how the outputs are generated from the inputs. (See Tom DeMarco's *Structured Analysis and System Specification* [Prentice Hall, 1985] to learn more about this kind of process specification.) That's because on a data-flow diagram (DFD), we match input and output data flows from parent to child. Note that we don't identify many objects from it. (That's what domain modeling, use case analysis, and robustness analysis are for!)

Requirements Traceability

Thanks to Jeff Kantor of ICONIX for the bulk of the following discussion.

When you look forward in the lifecycle, you perform *allocation* of requirements to use cases, classes, operations, states, and so forth. When you look backward, as you would in a verification/validation phase of the project, the term *traceability* comes into play. The two terms are different perspectives on the same relationship, but you traverse the relationship from each perspective under different circumstances.

When you move from analysis to design, you perform allocation in order to assign requirements to the design elements that will satisfy them. When you test and integrate code, your concern is with traceability, to determine which requirements led to each piece of code, and to provide criteria for testing that code. Thus allocation/traceability is a concern across the entire lifecycle, not just from system requirements to software requirements, but from software requirements to preliminary design, from preliminary design to detailed design, and from detailed design to implementation, testing, and integration.

You need to address several aspects of the allocation/traceability problem before you start serious coding.

Data capture has to do with finding efficient ways to capture the analytical elements of each phase of the lifecycle (requirements, functional analysis, functional allocation, hardware/software design, code, test, documentation, data) and the allocation/traceability relationships among these elements. You also need to consider how you will manage this information over several iterations of the lifecycle phase activities, and how you will manage updates and changes to the elements and relationships.

Data analysis and reduction encompasses ensuring that all the trace/allocation pointers are valid, that all requirements are allocated, and that all requirements trace. This aspect also presents management questions as iterative and incremental development occurs. In addition, you need to be aware of the impacts that changes have on elements throughout the system, and work to ensure that the results leave your design consistent with the users' needs.

Data reporting involves the ability to report efficiently on the results of data capture and data analysis/reduction. This typically takes the form of large tables that should be included in ongoing project documentation.

My CD-ROM tutorial, *Rose 98 for Power Users* (see **http://www.iconixsw.com/Rose98CD.html**), contains a discussion of how to extend Rational Rose to capture this information, along with some useful scripts.

Extending a Visual Modeling Tool to Support Requirements

You might expect that requirements were important enough that modern visual modeling tools would have built-in support for allocation and traceability "out of the box." Unfortunately, this is not always the case. Sometimes, we need to take matters into our own hands.

The following are pieces of a property file that you can use in automating the linking of named requirements with use cases and classes. (This file is available on my Rose 98 CD.)

```
(object Attribute
   tool    "Requirements"
   name    "default__Class"
   value   (list Attribute_Set
     (object Attribute
       tool  "Requirements"
       name  "REQ1"
       value "")
(object Attribute
   tool    "Requirements"
   name    "default__UseCase"
   value   (list Attribute_Set
     (object Attribute
       tool  "Requirements"
       name  "REQ1"
       value "")
```

Figure 7-3 shows a Requirements tab that will appear on your use case and class specifications within Rose using this property file (also available on the CD-ROM).

Figure 7-3 *Requirements Tab Within Rational Rose*

Requirements and the ICONIX Approach

You should address user requirements in conjunction with each of your work products from analysis and design, as described in Chapters 2 through 5 (and optionally, Chapter 6).

1. Review the allocations you made of requirements to use cases, using your original use case diagrams and your robustness diagrams. Each requirement should be allocated to at least one use case.

2. Verify that each requirement is addressed by at least one class in your static model.

3. Track requirement-level use case descriptions to actual designs on your sequence diagrams. Verify that the requirements are satisfied, one use case at a time.

4. If you've produced collaboration diagrams and/or state diagrams, ensure that you can trace the behavior that those diagrams model to specific requirements.

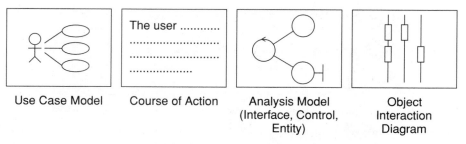

| Use Case Model | Course of Action | Analysis Model (Interface, Control, Entity) | Object Interaction Diagram |

Figure 7-4 *Traceability*

You may wonder whether this is overkill or whether only, say, big aerospace companies need to trace requirements, especially to this level of detail. I can see how you might think that.

Let me shed some light by telling you a true story about a training workshop that found me with a small team (about five developers) and a tight deadline.

The project had about 30 named requirements. We had allocated them to the use cases during analysis, and we were in the process of verifying that our sequence diagrams met those requirements. Suddenly, as we were tracing the first requirement, the lead engineer got, well, red in the face with embarrassment and said: "I just coded this last night, and I completely forgot about that exception condition."

It can happen to you, too.

Figure 7-4 illustrates an additional aspect of traceability.

This diagram shows that *each work product of the dynamic model is a direct and immediate consequence of the step that precedes it*. There are no leaps of faith between analysis and design. I believe this idea is Jacobson's most significant contribution to OO theory *and practice*. My fear that it is getting lost in the midst of the UML and the RUP is a key reason I decided to write this book.

Getting Ready to Code

It's only when you can account for every user requirement somewhere in your detailed design that you should feel comfortable proceeding with implementation.

This is how you should make that happen.

1. Make a list of requirements.
2. Write the user manual for the system, in the form of use cases.
3. Iterate with your customers until you have closure of items 1 and 2.
4. Make sure you can explicitly trace *every* piece of your design to at least one user requirement, and that you can trace *every* requirement to the point at which it's satisfied within your design. (See Figure 7-5.)
5. Trace your design back to your requirements as you review the design during your critical design review (see Figure 7-6).

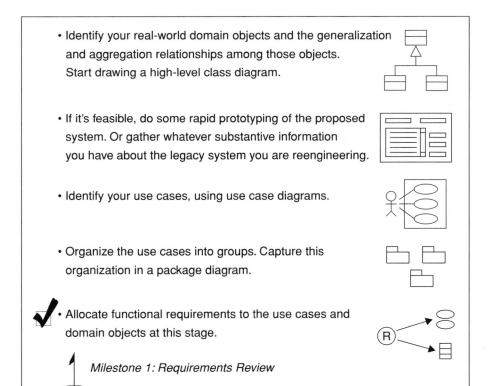

• Identify your real-world domain objects and the generalization and aggregation relationships among those objects. Start drawing a high-level class diagram.

• If it's feasible, do some rapid prototyping of the proposed system. Or gather whatever substantive information you have about the legacy system you are reengineering.

• Identify your use cases, using use case diagrams.

• Organize the use cases into groups. Capture this organization in a package diagram.

• Allocate functional requirements to the use cases and domain objects at this stage.

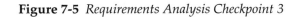

Milestone 1: Requirements Review

Figure 7-5 *Requirements Analysis Checkpoint 3*

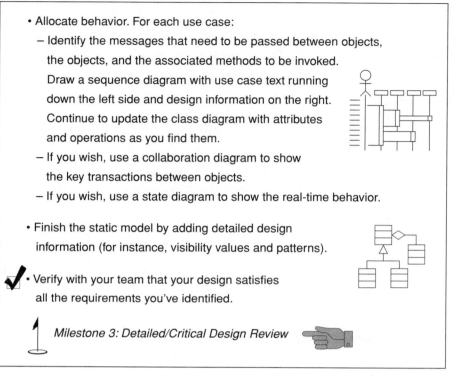

- Allocate behavior. For each use case:
  - Identify the messages that need to be passed between objects, the objects, and the associated methods to be invoked. Draw a sequence diagram with use case text running down the left side and design information on the right. Continue to update the class diagram with attributes and operations as you find them.
  - If you wish, use a collaboration diagram to show the key transactions between objects.
  - If you wish, use a state diagram to show the real-time behavior.

- Finish the static model by adding detailed design information (for instance, visibility values and patterns).

- Verify with your team that your design satisfies all the requirements you've identified.

  Milestone 3: Detailed/Critical Design Review

Figure 7-6 *Design Checkpoint 2*

Top 10 Things You Shall Remember About Requirements

10. *The project team shall make as complete a list of requirements as possible, as early in the project as it can, rather than start off with code.*

9. *REPEAT AFTER ME: Requirements are requirements; use cases are use cases. Requirements are not use cases; use cases are not requirements.*

8. *There are several types of requirements, including functional requirements, performance requirements, and constraints.*

7. *The project team should demonstrate connection of at least one use case directly with each requirement during requirements review.*

6. *The project team should demonstrate connection of at least one class directly with each requirement during requirements review.*

5. *The use case model shall serve as a collection of mini-contracts between developers and the sponsors of the new system. Each use case shall serve as both input to the development process and as a user-acceptance test case.*

4. *The team shall trace the allocation of requirements to use cases and domain classes as part of the requirements review.*

3. *The text of each use case "contract" must appear on a sequence diagram so that the development team is constantly reminded of the "contractual requirements" they're working against as they do the design.*

2. *The detailed design, as reflected in your sequence diagrams, shall be defended against the use case text as part of design review.*

1. *There shall be at least one test case in place to verify each requirement.*

Chapter 8

Implementation

Implementation is not the major focus of this book. for three reasons.

1. If you've done a good job with your analysis and design, coding should be straightforward, as long as you continue to keep a close eye on your users' requirements. (In other words, the die is cast, for the most part, by the time you get here.)

2. There are enough available object-oriented programming books to last several lifetimes, and I see no reason to add to the mix.

3. Coding issues tend to be language-specific, even compiler-specific.

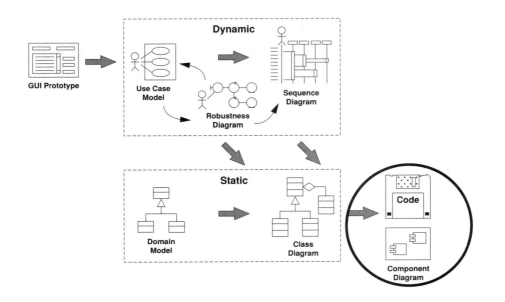

I can, however, offer advice on related issues, as well as some sample code headers that correspond with one of our sequence diagrams.

Project Staffing Issues

Your project will likely have small subteams within the larger team structure. It would make sense to have each subteam address one chunk of the system you're building (that is, a package of use cases), from initial analysis through delivery.

From my experience, what works best is a mix of senior and junior people on each subteam, with a senior person with particularly strong experience serving as the lead. This enables you to spread your talent around; the less-experienced people can learn from the veterans while they infuse a high level of energy and enthusiasm.

I'm not generally in the business of defining specific roles that team members should play, but I have noticed a few tendencies in my years of consulting and teaching.

- Database folks are usually more oriented toward static class modeling. Make sure they don't just replicate the database schema and pass it off as a class diagram, as they occasionally tend to want to do. (Refer back to Chapter 2, as necessary. Have them read the Wirfs-Brock book, too [Prentice Hall, 1990].)

- GUI programmers usually relate better to use cases. However, you need to make sure they don't get lost in GUI design along the way. Also, technical writers with user guide experience can be valuable for writing use cases, because they are accustomed to describing system usage.

- System programmers should focus on such things as performance issues and state and collaboration diagrams.

- Senior OOA&D people should do the sequence diagrams, if possible. If junior folks do them, the senior people *must* review them (and vice versa, interestingly enough).

To maximize your resources, have your senior people review the work that the more inexperienced people have done, while the latter get started on another part of the system. And, if you can manage to have domain expertise represented on each subteam or enlist the services of such people as class librarians (who can identify reuse possibilities) and user liaisons (who can stand in for your users on an as-needed basis), so much the better.

Project Management

There aren't quite as many books about software project management as there are about object-oriented programming (OOP), but there are still more than enough. In the face of that, I've reduced my advice on this matter to the following.

- *Hire smart people, then **stay out of their way**.* The number-one cause of project failure is managerial interference, primarily political. If you've put together strong subteams, let them perform. (In other words, don't act like the pointy-haired boss in *Dilbert*.)

- *Don't lose your focus on the process.* It will probably be tempting to ignore class diagrams instead of updating them to reflect new knowledge gleaned from coding, or to jump into integration testing without doing rigorous unit testing first. This would not be wise; it may cost you dearly later in the project.

- ***Don't expect a visual modeling tool to generate foolproof code.*** The code you get out of a tool is meant as a starting point for real programmers—programmers who have reasonable experience working with the language the code is written in, that is. In most cases, you will get only class headers. Unrealistic expectations of automagic code generation are responsible for a depressingly large percentage of visual-modeling-tool sales—and an even more depressing shelfware-to-sales ratio. (In other words, if it sounds too good to be true, it probably is.)

- *Don't mistake **quantity** of generated code for **quality**.* The following is a small part of the get/set code I generated from our example system. (Rose generated about 15 pages of this stuff for two or three classes.)

```
/**
   Get operation for the claimSubmit attribute
     (generated).
   @roseuid 362CF94002C6
   */
```

```
public void getclaimSubmit() {
}

/**
Set operation for the claimSubmit attribute
  (generated).
@roseuid 362CF9400370
*/
public void setclaimSubmit(value) {
}

/**
Get operation for the discountPercent attribute
  (generated).
@roseuid 362CF94502C6
*/
public void getdiscountPercent() {
}

/**
Set operation for the discountPercent attribute
  (generated).
@roseuid 362CF9450366
*/
public void setdiscountPercent(value) {
}
```

Exciting stuff, isn't it?

Revisiting the Static Model

By now, you will have finished all your sequence diagrams and refined your static model to a great extent. If you were careful, your methods are small and atomic, which are signs of a good design.

Before you move ahead, you need to do two more tasks that involve the static model.

1. Define argument lists for your operations (for example, those involving data typing).
2. Define operation logic.

If you don't mind, I'll leave these as exercises for the reader.

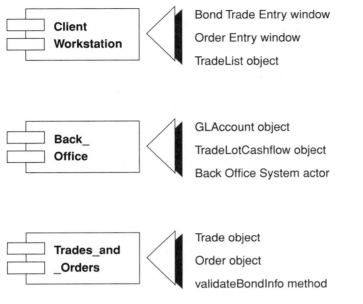

Figure 8-1 *Component Diagram*

Allocating Classes to Components

The last step that's required before you begin coding involves assigning your classes to **components**. These are the physical parts of a system that "realize" the conceptual elements you've defined to this point.

Figure 8-1 shows the key components of our example system, along with some elements that belong to each component.

Code Headers

A tool like Rational Rose can generate large volumes of code in many languages. But none of this code will be algorithmic in nature. Because I'm a strong advocate of visual modeling tools (including Rose), and because the algorithmic code is generally the most interesting, and because this book isn't about OOP, I won't show you any real code. I

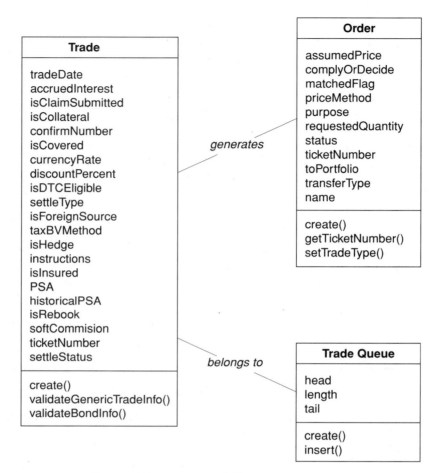

Figure 8-2 *Design-Level Class Diagram Excerpt*

will, however, show you some material to help you trace our generated code back through the example model.

Figure 8-2 shows those elements of the fully updated static class model that are relevant to the Enter Buy Trade use case.

Figure 8-3 shows the sequence diagram we drew for that use case and excerpts from the associated headers of the classes corresponding to the objects on this diagram.

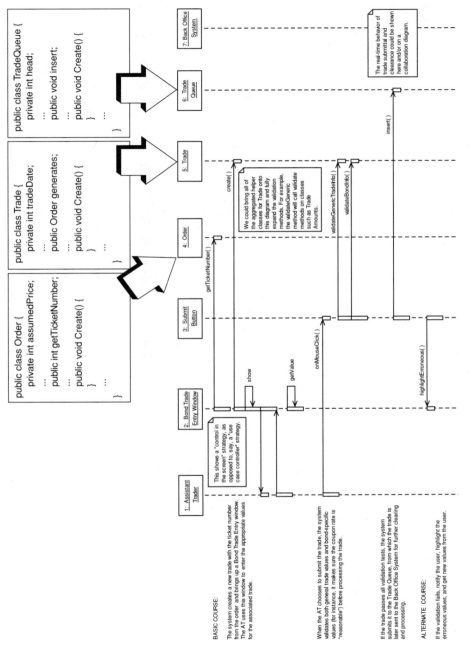

Figure 8-3 *Enter Buy Trade Sequence Diagram with Headers*

Testing

You should look at testing as a full member of the iterative and incremental development lifecycle, not just as something you occasionally do after you've cranked out a bunch of code. Begin testing on a piece of your new system as soon as you've built a reasonable implementation of the detailed design of that piece. As pieces evolve, you can test on a larger scale while continuing to operate iteratively on each piece.

Because use cases have driven everything else we've discussed to this point, it only makes sense that I recommend that you drive a healthy portion of testing with your use cases. In particular, I suggest you treat each use case as a unit within **black-box testing**, which involves basing test cases on the externally visible behavior of the unit.

This is, in fact, *user-acceptance testing* within our approach. The use case is what we said the system would do; if the system passes the test that uses the use case as its scenario, then we can say that the system actually does what we said it would do.

With this approach, you'll have at least one test for the basic course of action and at least one test for each alternative course. Every test will have a unique identifier so that you can keep track of it in the larger scheme of things, just as you do for a use case or a class. You also tie these test cases into your requirements as you go. (Refer to Chapter 7 to reinforce this principle.)

White-box testing involves testing the internal structure of the methods that belong to each class to make sure they do what you think they should do. Building good sets of test cases for this kind of testing requires as high a level of diligence as any analysis or design task. You need to perform unit testing for every method within every class, following as many paths as possible along the way.

If you have a real-time system (see Chapter 6), you should add **state-based testing** to the project. During this kind of testing, you monitor changes that take place in an object's attributes in order to test the interactions among that object's methods. You can use the elements on state diagrams as the basis for test cases.

Integration testing, then, involves testing logical groups (packages) of use cases at such time as those use cases have passed the unit testing phase. From there, it's a logical leap to full-blown system testing, within which you can do such things as stress testing (executing several use cases at the same time), full-scale testing (increasing key parameters to their established limits), and negative testing (going beyond those limits). Again, you should treat test cases within these test scenarios as separate entities that you can explicitly link with requirements—in particular, those that involve performance.

Bob Binder (**http://www.rbsc.com**) has assembled an extensive suite of information about OO testing.

Metrics

In his 1994 book, Booch discusses several metrics that can be used for object-oriented systems. I talked about two concepts related to metrics, cohesion and coupling, in Chapter 5. I think they're the most important ones. The other four can be revealing, however, in that they can expose potential weaknesses in your design, and likely spots for groups of errors. Chris Kemerer and his colleagues at MIT are the originators of these (read Kemerer's *Software Project Management: Readings and Cases* [Richard D. Irwin, 1996]).

1. *Weighted methods per class* is a measure of the complexity of your classes. In its simplest form, this amounts to the number of methods in each class. It's safe to say that a class that has a significantly larger number than the average is more likely to have problems.

2. *Response for a class* is a measure of the number of methods a class's instances can call. Just as an outsize number of methods in a class might indicate a problem, a class with a relatively high number of messages going out to other classes could lead to problems down the road.

3. *Depth of inheritance tree* is a measure of the *shape* of your static model. If you have more than a few layers in your tree, it may be difficult to track process and data flows.

4. *Number of children* is a measure of the *size* of your static model. I suggest you aim for balance in this area relative to the depth of your tree, as described previously.

The following are excerpts from a metrics script available on the Rose 98 CD.

```
Sub PrintAttribute (anAttribute As Attribute, Indent As
  Integer)
    If Len (anAttribute.Documentation) > 0 Then
      Print
      call PrintDocumentation (anAttribute.Documentation,
        Indent)
    End If
    Print Space$(Indent) + anAttribute.Type + "" +
      anAttribute.Name;
     If Len (anAttribute.InitValue) > 0 Then
       Print " = "+ anAttribute.InitValue;
     End If
     Print ";"
End Sub


Sub PrintClassRoles (aClass As Class, Indent As Integer)
    Dim theRoles As RoleCollection
    Dim theRole As Role

    Set theRoles = aClass.GetRoles ()
    For i% = 1 To theRoles.Count
      Set theRole = theRoles.GetAt (i%)
      Print Space$(Indent);
      If Len (theRole.Name) > 0 Then
        Print theRole.Name
      Else
        Print "<Not Named>"
      End If
    Next i%
End Sub
```

Figure 8-4 shows some of the results of running that metrics script on our example system. (Brooks Van Horn of TRW wrote this script. Like the other scripts in this book, it's available on my Rose 98 CD.)

As you can see from the numbers—in particular, the 0.2 operations per class—our example is clearly a long way from a finished product (after

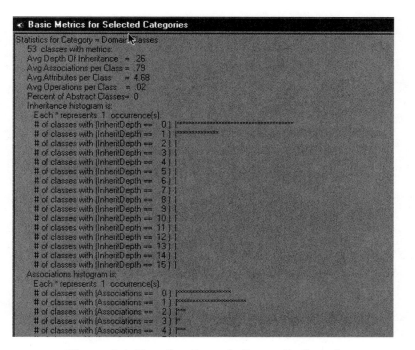

Figure 8-4 *How Our Example System Performed*

all, we've only worked through two use cases), but at least you get the idea of what kind of metrics are useful.

Of course, it's always a good idea to track the rate at which bugs are exposed. If you were reasonably rigorous in your analysis and design, you shouldn't have large numbers of bugs, even at the beginning of each increment of your unit testing. But you should expect to see more bugs up front within each test cycle than later on in the cycle. It's also worth noting that the chances of finding bugs in a piece of code are significantly higher than normal if you've already found lots of bugs in that code. (Maurice Howard Halstead had some enlightening things to say about this in his 1977 book *Elements of Software Science*; unfortunately, it's out of print.) Along those lines, you should make sure you know who's writing what code.

Tracking Use Case Driven Development

The following is another script from my Rose 98 CD you can use *before* you embark on code to generate an Excel spreadsheet that shows which robustness diagrams and sequence diagrams have been completed.

```
Sub Main()
Dim theCat As Category
Dim theModel As Model
Dim allUseCases As UseCaseCollection
Dim the UseCase as UseCase

Set ExcelApp = CreateObject("Excel.Application")
ExcelApp.Visible = True
Set WorkBook = ExcelApp.Application.Workbooks.Add
Set WorkSheet = Workbook.WorkSheets.Add

WorkSheet.Name = "Excel"
WorkSheet.Cells(1,1).Value = "Use Case"
WorkSheet.Cells(1,2).Value = "has Robustness Diagram"
WorkSheet.Cells(1,3).Value = "has Sequence Diagram"

row = 2
Set theModel = RoseApp.CurrentModel
For i = 1 To theModel.GetAllUseCases.Count
    row = row + 1
    Set theUseCase = theModel.GetAllUseCases.GetAt(i)
    WorkSheet.Cells(row,1).Value = theUseCase.name
    If theUseCase.ClassDiagrams.Count > 0
        Then WorkSheet.Cells(row,2).Value = "YES"
    If theUseCase.ScenarioDiagrams.Count > 0
        Then WorkSheet.Cells(row,3).Value = "YES"
Next i

End Sub
```

Figure 8-5 shows what happened when I ran this script for our example system.

	A	B	C	D	E
1	Use Case	has Robustness Diagram	has Sequence Diagram		
2					
3	Enter Sell Trade	YES			
4	Generate Portfolio Report				
5	Enter Buy Trade	YES	YES		
6	Enter Investment				
7	Aggregate Portfolios				
8	Define Investment				
9	Perform Order Entry	YES	YES		
10	Perform Trade Adjustment	YES			
11	View Portfolio				
12	Create New Portfolio				
13					

Figure 8-5 *Tracking Our Example System's Diagrams*

Wrapping Up

Figure 8-6 shows where we are. (*Delivery* is such a satisfying word!)

If you've followed my advice to this point, you have a working system with sound architecture. So, go find your boss and demand a raise!

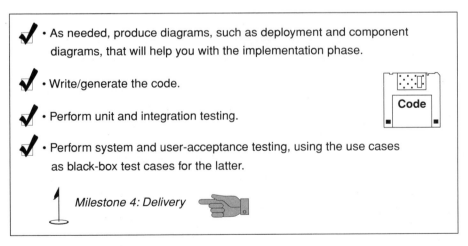

- • As needed, produce diagrams, such as deployment and component diagrams, that will help you with the implementation phase.

- • Write/generate the code.

- • Perform unit and integration testing.

- • Perform system and user-acceptance testing, using the use cases as black-box test cases for the latter.

Milestone 4: Delivery

Figure 8-6 *Implementation Checkpoint 1*

Top 10 Ways to Mess Up Your Project Despite Doing Good OOA&D

10. *Bet the farm by doing your most critical project as your first effort that involves object-oriented development.*

9. *Make sure there's nobody with any OO experience on your project team.*

8. *Don't do unit testing on a class-by-class basis. Instead, go directly into integration testing and hope for the best.*

7. *Keep most of your senior designers busy writing use cases; have your junior people work on the sequence diagrams.*

6. *Don't bother to review any of your analysis or design models.*

5. *Keep your design model completely segregated from your use case model; we all know that use cases don't affect code.*

4. *Implement the easy parts of your system first. Leave the critical items for the end, near the deadline. (You can earn lots of overtime pay this way!)*

3. *Take a team of 20 or so Visual Basic programmers, hand them a C++ compiler and a visual modeling tool, and leave them to their own devices.*

2. *Ignore the analysis and design models you've produced, write the code, and reverse-engineer all the code you've written into an as-built object model. Your clients will never know the difference, right?*

1. *Assume your visual modeling tool will generate great code for you, and hire a bunch of junior college students (none CS majors) to handle coding.*

Appendix

"Uses" vs. "Extends"

The Object Technology User Group (OTUG) is a valuable forum for comparing notes with other smart people about object-oriented subjects. However, things can get pretty silly (or worse) when people spend too much time focusing on minutiae, as you're about to see.

Note that I've edited the following postings for readability.

Two excerpts state the fundamental problem in particularly eloquent terms.

1. I don't know about you guys, but I think I have spent as much time on understanding and applying uses and extends as I have spent on the rest of the UML.

2. Few people at all appear to understand the difference between uses and extends.

Posts that contained such cries for help caused some people to offer what appeared to be, at least on the surface, reasonable explanations. For instance:

The distinction of uses vs. extends seems very clear and very relevant: it's all a matter of integration. The extends construct informs the developer that the integration between use cases is one to one. The uses construct informs the developer that the integration is one to many.

When deciding between the uses and extends constructs, I usually ask the question: How many use cases will be calling this use case? If the answer is one, then I use extends. If the answer is many, then I use uses.

Others, however, took entirely different views on the subject, such as:

> The choice between uses and extends has little to do with how many other use cases are involved. Rather, it has to do with which use case knows about which other. In the uses case, the using use case knows about the used use case. This is very much like a function call; many "using" use cases can "use" a used use case. [Try saying *that* fast three times in a row.] In the extends case, however, the extended use case contains the primary course of events, but has no idea of the existence of the extending use case.

> The extending use case overrides sections of the extended use case. Thus, the extending use case acts kind of like an editor, changing only certain parts of the extended use case. So, when the extended use case changes, all of the extending use cases inherit those changes without being affected.

This kind of reasoning is just too complicated for most people to follow, let alone do anything constructive with. And then we have:

> If you look at this from the perspective of "usage instance," then an instance that follows the flow of the initial use case and the extending use case is really a member of the subset of all instances that follow the flow of the initial use case only. We've informally started calling the initial use case in this example the "covering use case."

Now there's new terminology to learn: "usage instance" and "covering use case." I think use case modeling should be *fairly easy to do*, especially in the face of the hard stuff, such as sequence diagramming; efforts to make it complicated give me a headache.

The likes of those last two posts went a long way toward helping me decide to try to shift the focus of the (by now, *really* big) thread to precedes and invokes. This next text is from one of my posts; it sums up my thoughts about uses and extends—and, come to think of it, about use case driven modeling in general.

> Invokes is not defined in the UML specs, but, along with its partner precedes, comes from the OML. Some of us prefer this set of relationships to uses/extends for the following reasons:
>
> • Uses/extends carries baggage associated with multiple definitions of the terms. (I almost wrote "n-ary polymorphic definitions," but I stopped myself just in

time.) My characterization of the debate associated with which term is proper remains "generates much heat, little light."

- The additional semantic distinction that differentiates uses from extends is of questionable value. For the purposes of driving object models from use cases, it is of exceedingly small value. On the other hand, the confusion caused by using these terms is fairly high, and the accompanying slowdown in modeling that comes from making uses/extends decisions, as opposed to just using invokes, is problematic.

- Another instance of "negative value added" can be found if we examine who the consumers of the use case models are. In many cases—we hope—use case models are reviewed by non-technical folks, including marketing people, and in some cases actual end users of the system. These folks are almost certain not to understand the subtle distinctions between uses and extends, and are almost certain to be confused by them instead. Since one of the main purposes of the use case model is to elicit end user validation on how the proposed system will work, confusing these people is generally a bad idea.

Somewhere along the line, however, some people got the idea that I was (a) a UML heretic (I talked about this in Chapter 1, remember?) and (b) ignorant about how extends works. Consider this:

> Folks, just because everybody's doing it doesn't mean it's right. Invokes is, and maybe rightly so, a shortcut in the good old American tradition that led to rusting gas-guzzlers that ran "OK" back in the '70s...until Japanese imports came along.

> For many folks, "close enough is good enough," and they're going to be moving on to new projects so others can come in and mop up and try to figure out what their "version" of the UML really means. I guess it's like moving obscure, poorly documented code up one level to the model! I've watched these threads for months and I *still* don't know what is so overwhelmingly unfathomable about uses and extends!

Then there's this:

> If you guys want to use invokes, then fine—don't conform to suggested UML usage and predefined stereotypes. March to

> the beat of a different drummer; *after all, this is America.* [Emphasis added for dramatic effect.] However, please don't imply that the rest of us who want to follow the UML standard and want to be as precise and unambiguous as possible are wrong.

> The OOSE book (if not the UML spec) puts forth very clear definitions for uses and extends, and they're what we follow. Invokes is just a bit too generalized for us. I'm glad it works for you.

Well, I'm glad that at least one person thinks the definitions of uses and extends are "very clear."

Don't get me wrong. I certainly understand the differences between uses and extends; I just don't happen to have any use for extends, and in fact, I find its use to be counterproductive.

Here's another one of my attempts to steer the discussion back to the issue of *building good models*:

> All that any of these three constructs (uses, extends, invokes) are, to me, are ways to factor out commonality in usage when doing a scenario-based decomposition. If you don't have a mechanism for factoring out commonality, you wind up with a bunch of redundant, in-line text in the course of action for your use cases.

> As these courses of action form the basis for the sequence diagrams that follow, it's important that there isn't a lot of redundant overlap in the use case text. Anything beyond that qualifies as Shakespearean modeling (*Much Ado About Nothing*) in my mind, because the reuse that everybody is looking for generally comes out of the design activity that takes place on the sequence diagrams.

Alas, there are among us those who insist on continuing to muddy the waters.

> There is a substantial difference between uses and extends. There seems to be no difference whatever between uses and invokes. The value of extends is very high, since it allows use case X to be extended without modification (i.e., the open-closed principle).

Use Cases, the Extends Relationship, and Code

That mention of the "open-closed principle," and the fact that around that time, a number of other people mentioned things like "if" statements in the context of use cases, prompts me to offer the following, which I haven't posted to OTUG (yet).

References to programming constructs such as "if" statements lead me to believe that many programmers—and, for that matter, some tool vendors—have some fundamental misconceptions about use cases.

Nowhere in the last 150 or so pages have I suggested that anybody should take the text of a use case and attempt to code it in, say, C++. That is to say, *usage scenarios are fundamentally different from pseudocode*, even though they're both written in English. An "if" statement in a user manual might read as follows: "If you want to cancel the current transaction, click the Cancel button." There's nothing particularly harmful about expressing user behavior this way.

The open-closed principle reference is another example of someone attempting to applying programming principles, or at least software design principles, to writing use cases. The problem with doing this is that *use cases are not code*, and the principles that guide the design of good code are not necessarily the best principles for guiding the design of good use cases (just as the principles of freestyle swimming don't work particularly well when it comes to riding a bicycle). For example: when we write code, being terse and efficient is a good thing; when we write use case text, for the purpose of discovering objects, among other things, it is better to be a bit more verbose, with the goal of completely and unambiguously describing everything the users of the new system will be able to do.

Bob Martin offers a good discussion of the open-closed principle on page 109 of his book *Designing Object-Oriented C++ Applications: Using the Booch Method* (Prentice Hall, 1995). This is a good principle to follow when designing software; it's related to the idea of *closing* a function to *modification* while leaving it *open* for *extension*. (If you're getting use cases confused with functions at this point, go back and read Chapter 7 again.) This idea is likely related to the UML's extends relationship. In fact, the UML's *extension points* construct involves denoting places where a use case can be extended.

Martin describes the benefits of following the open-closed principle as follows:

> Why is this important? Why should we want to close functions against modification? Clearly, if we can really close a function, then we will never have to modify it! This is quite a goal.
>
> If we can close all the functions in a system, then we can extend and enhance that system without making changes to working code. Instead, all changes will be made by adding new code. If you don't have to change a function in order to enhance it, then you don't have to read it, either.
>
> You don't have to understand how the function works. All you have to understand is what it expects from the virtual functions that it calls. Ideally, then, extending an existing software system, in which all of the functions are closed, involves no changes to existing working code, and no reading of that code either.

Now, these are wonderful principles to work with, and goals to strive for, when we're designing code. Generally speaking, reading code isn't much fun (except to a certain technical writer, who shall remain nameless); I'd go so far as to say that it's something that most developers will go to great lengths to avoid doing. Ripping up code that's already been built and debugged is even less fun. However—repeat after me, please—*use cases are not code*.

Use cases are much closer, conceptually, to user manuals than they are to code. When we're doing a development project using the approach I describe within these covers, we're not trying to minimize rework of already built stuff—we're *trying to build a system that the client wants us to build*. That means that trying to design use cases so they don't ever need to be read is simply *wrong*.

Use cases have to be designed so they can be easily read and understood by non-technical users and marketing folks who have never come near a UML book. And the designs that we come up with (which, repeat after me again, if you'd be so kind, are *not* the use cases) need to be verified against those use cases in order for us to make sure that we've met our users' requirements.

What's more, in order to build use case models that serve the purposes I describe in this book, a single method of factoring out commonality (using invokes, for example) is sufficient. The way I see it, you need extends if you are organizing your use cases the same way you organize code—but unfortunately, this is simply the wrong way to organize use cases.

Back to OTUG

After reading about the open-closed principle on OTUG, I subsequently demonstrated (not for the first time) that I could express use case factoring with uses (or invokes) alone, and that I could live without extends very nicely. Then this appeared:

> The proponents of dropping extends are really asking you to drop software engineering principles and nothing more—all under the fallacious guise that it is somehow easier for a user to filter through a bunch of "if" statements and make unnecessary changes to use cases that would never be necessary had these proponents learned how to use extends and teach their customers the same (which can be done in a matter of minutes).
>
> I'm really disappointed with a few of you so-called experts pushing politics over sound software engineering principles.

This, ladies and gentlemen, is what's known in the world of the Internet as a *flame*. If this were the 1860s, I would say something like, "Them's fightin' words, mister."

The following was my response to all posts along the same lines.

> I use invokes and precedes because in my experience, they make more sense, are less confusing, and are more effective. The resulting use case models are better structured, and easier to understand, in my opinion. I am not stupid; I understand the semantics of extends and uses. I am not an agent of the OML. I have no political agenda. My opinion on the subject is a reasonably informed one, based on an acceptable level of experience. The *only* reason I use these constructs is that they work better, in my experience.

The moral of the story: *Use what works for you* and don't be intimidated by "true believers."

Bibliography

Grady Booch: *Object-Oriented Analysis and Design with Applications, Second Edition*. Addison-Wesley, 1994.

Grady Booch, James Rumbaugh, and Ivar Jacobson: *The Unified Modeling Language User Guide*. Addison Wesley Longman, 1999.

Peter DeGrace and Leslie Hulet Stahl: *The Olduvai Imperative*. Prentice Hall, 1993.

Tom DeMarco: *Structured Analysis and System Specification*. Prentice Hall, 1985.

Kurt Derr: *Applying OMT*. SIGS Books, 1995.

Bruce Powel Douglass: *Real-Time UML: Developing Efficient Objects for Embedded Systems*. Addison Wesley Longman, 1998.

Erich Gamma, Richard Helm, Ralph Johnson, and John Vlissides [Gang of Four]: *Design Patterns: Elements of Reusable Object-Oriented Software*. Addison-Wesley, 1995.

Maurice Howard Halstead: *Elements of Software Science*. 1977. Out of print.

Ivar Jacobson, Magnus Christerson, Patrik Jonsson, and Gunnar Övergaard: *Object-Oriented Software Engineering: A Use Case Driven Approach*. Addison-Wesley, 1992.

Ivar Jacobson, Maria Ericsson, and Agneta Jacobson: *The Object Advantage: Business Process Reengineering with Object Technology*. Addison-Wesley, 1995.

Chris Kemerer: *Software Project Management: Readings and Cases*. Richard D. Irwin, 1996.

Robert Cecil Martin: *Designing Object-Oriented C++ Applications: Using the Booch Method*. Prentice Hall, 1995.

Doug Rosenberg: "Applying O-O Methods to Interactive Multimedia Projects," *OBJECT*, June 1995.

Doug Rosenberg: *Mastering UML with Rational Rose* (CD-ROM; ICONIX, 1997).

Doug Rosenberg: "Modeling Client/Server Systems," *OBJECT*, March 1994.

Doug Rosenberg: *An Object Methodology Overview* (CD-ROM; ICONIX, 1994).

Doug Rosenberg: *Rational Rose 98 for Power Users* (CD-ROM; ICONIX, 1998).

Doug Rosenberg: "UML Applied: Nine Tips to Incorporating UML into Your Project," *Software Development*, March 1998.

Doug Rosenberg: *A Unified Object Modeling Approach* (2 CD-ROM set; ICONIX, 1996).

Doug Rosenberg: "Using the Object Modeling Technique with Objectory for Client/Server Development," *OBJECT*, November 1993.

Doug Rosenberg: "Validating the Design of Client/Server Systems," *OBJECT*, July 1994.

Doug Rosenberg and Kendall Scott: "Optimizing Rose 98 to Support Use Case Driven Object Modeling." Available at **http://www.rosearch-itect.com/mag/archives/9810/online.shtml**.

James Rumbaugh, Michael Blaha, William Premerlani, Frederick Eddy, and William Lorenzen: *Object-Oriented Modeling and Design*. Prentice Hall, 1991.

William Shakespeare: *Much Ado About Nothing*. Public domain.

Rebecca Wirfs-Brock, Brian Wilkerson, and Lauren Wiener: *Designing Object-Oriented Software*. Prentice Hall, 1990.

Index

A

activity diagram
  and state diagram 116
  defined 116
actor
  adding to sequence diagram 91, 92
  defined 39
  notation 39
  robustness diagram rules 69
aggregation
  and helper classes 27
  defined 25
  examples 26
Alger/Goldstein method 4
alternate course of action
  and testing 142
  capturing 48
  defined 48
  examples 52, 53, 54
analysis paralysis
  alerts 20, 24, 25, 45, 49, 50, 66, 76, 82,
    85, 102, 110, 114
  introduction 8
  top 10 list 119
analysis-level use case
  defined 40
  examples 54
applicability 96
architect's rendering 103
association class
  defined 26
  developing 26
  notation 27

associations
  and verbs 16
  building 23
  defined 23
  notation 24
asynchronous message type 111
attributes
  adding to domain model 75
  and nouns 16
  and possessive phrases 16
  finalizing on classes 101
automagic 85, 92, 137
autopilot 9

B

balking message type 111
basic course of action
  and testing 142
  defined 47
  examples 47, 51, 53, 54
  getting started 48
behavior allocation
  and CRC cards 95
  and quality of classes 96
  critical nature 95
  initial definition 82
  what not to do 82
Bennett, Doug 82
best of breed 4, 5
Billy Bob 124
black-box testing 142
Booch, Grady xvi, 1, 3, 4, 5, 6, 7, 25, 83,
    96, 104, 110, 111, 143, 157

booster-stage engine 76
bouncing back and forth 41
boundary objects
    adding to sequence diagram 89, 91
    and alternative courses of action 66
    conventions 64
    defined 66
    finding 66
    introduction 61
    notation 68
    robustness diagram rules 69
    validation logic 66
bug exposure rate 145
business process use case 40
business rule processing 83

C

candidate associations 23, 24
candidate classes 17, 19, 20
capacity requirements 122
cement collar 6
changing of the guard 82
child 21
class
    defined 17
    discovering 17, 19
    notations 21
    sources 17
class diagram
    analysis-level 32, 77, 78
    design-level 105, 140
    examples 29, 31
Class-Responsibility-Collaboration
    (CRC) cards
    See CRC cards
cohesion 103
collaboration diagram
    and requirements 129
    defined 110
    example 112
    notation 111
    personnel 136
    versus sequence diagram 110, 111
    when to use 109
completeness 103

complexity 96
component
    allocating classes 139
    defined 139
component diagram 139
composition 25
concrete use case 40
connecting tissue 67
continuous improvement 20, 53
continuous refinement 65, 74
contractual agreement 87
control objects
    and sequence diagram 94, 98
    as placeholders 67
    conventions 68
    defined 67
    introduction 61
    notation 68
    robustness diagram rules 69
controllers
    and sequence diagram 94
    defined 67, 83
coupling 102
CRC cards 4, 95
Critical Design Review (CDR)
        milestone 13, 106, 132

D

data analysis and reduction 127
data capture 127
data flow diagram (DFD) 3, 116, 126
data reporting 127
data requirements 122
data-centered methods 3
Define Investment use case
    alternate course of action 53
    basic course of action 52
    introduction 52
DeGrace, Peter 123, 157
Delivery milestone 13, 147
DeMarco, Tom 9, 126, 157
depth of inheritance tree 143
Derr, Kurt 16, 33, 157
design patterns 104
design without the GUI 43

design-level use case 40
Dilbert 137
do event 113
domain model
    and associations 23
    and entity objects 65
    and field names 45
    and use case text 47
    as glossary 16, 33
    updating 74, 100, 138
domain modeling
    defined 15
    getting started 16
    personnel 136
Douglass, Bruce Powel 115, 157
Drink Beer use case 124
dumb servers 67
dynamic model
    essence 84
    getting started 38

E

Enter Buy Trade use case
    alternate course of action 70, 74
    basic course of action 53, 70, 73
    class diagram 140
    introduction 51
    robustness analysis 71
    robustness diagram 73
    sequence diagram 88, 90, 91, 97, 141
Enter Sell Trade use case
    alternate course of action 54
    basic course of action 54
    introduction 51
entity objects
    adding to sequence diagram 89, 90
    defined 67
    discovering 75
    finding 67
    introduction 61
    naming 65
    notation 68
    robustness diagram rules 69
entity-relationship diagram (ERD) 3, 23
entry event 113

error handling 83
event trace diagram 84
exit event 113
extends relationship 49, 117, 149, 150,
        152, 153, 155
extension points 153

F

Factory Method pattern 104
flame 155
flowchart 116
focus of control 84
function
    as vehicle 123
    examples 125
    vs. requirement 123
functional decomposition 117, 124, 126
functional requirements 122
Fusion 3

G

Gamma, Erich 104, 157
Gang of Four 157
generalization
    and use cases 49
    defined 21
    examples 22, 23
    notation 22
grammatical inspection 16, 20
graphical user interface (GUI)
    See GUI
guard 113
GUI
    and system behavior 41
    design without the GUI 43
    personnel 136
GUI-Repository-Logic 66

H

Halstead, Maurice Howard 145, 157
hamburger 33
Helm, Richard 104, 157
helper classes 27, 31

I

implementation knowledge 96
includes relationship 49
integration testing 143
interaction diagrams 82
interaction modeling
    defined 81
    finishing 105
    goals 82
invokes relationship 50, 57, 93, 150,
    151, 152, 155
is-a relationship 21
iterate and refine 33
iterative and incremental 6, 7, 10, 40,
    127
Iterator pattern 104

J

Jacobson, Ivar xvi, xviii, 2, 4, 5, 6, 7, 16,
    40, 61, 62, 63, 64, 68, 82, 83, 84, 92,
    110, 130, 157
Johnson, Ralph 104, 157

K

Kantor, Jeff 126
Kemerer, Chris 143, 158
kind-of relationship 21
Kitchen Sink 27

L

leaps of faith 130
less is more 8
light switch objects 114
link class 26
localizing changes 67

M

magic formula 63
Martin, Bob 153, 158
Martin/Odell method 3

messages
    numbering on collaboration
        diagram 112
    on sequence diagram 84, 97, 99
    parameters 96
Method of the Month Club 3
method types
    data-centered 3
    scenario-based 3, 4
    structural 3
Methodology 9
methods
    assigning to classes 93
    finalizing on classes 101
    on sequence diagram 84, 97,
        99
milestones
    Critical Design Review (CDR) 13
    Delivery 13
    introduction 10
    Preliminary Design Review 12
    Requirements Review 11
minimalist approach 7
mining 27, 45
mini-spec 126
Model-View-Controller 66
much heat, little light 151
multiplicity 24, 26

N

negative value added 151
number of children 143

O

Object Behavior Analysis (OBA) 4
object diagram 110
object glossary 65
object interaction diagram 82, 84
Object Modeling Technique (OMT)
    See OMT
Object Technology User Group
    (OTUG)
    See OTUG

Object-Oriented Software Engineering (OOSE)
   See OOSE
Objectory 2, 5, 62, 82
objects
   and nouns 16
   and possessive phrases 16
   on sequence diagram 84
OML 150, 155
OMT 3, 4, 5, 6, 16, 26, 84, 116
OOSE 4, 5, 6
open-closed principle 152, 153, 154, 155
operations
   and verbs 16
   on sequence diagram 84
opportunistic 6
OTUG 25, 50, 149

P

package 55, 136
package diagram 55, 56
Page-Jones, Meilir 43
parent 21
part-of relationship 25
patterns 104
peer review 74
Perform Order Entry use case
   alternate courses of action 52, 53, 70, 73
   basic course of action 52, 70, 71
   introduction 51
   robustness analysis 70
   robustness diagram 72
   sequence diagram 99
Perform Trade Adjustment use case 54
Perform Trade Entry use case 46, 47, 48, 51, 53
performance requirements 122
personality 94, 103
piece-part relationship 25
postcondition 50
precedes relationship 50, 57, 150, 155
precondition 50
preliminary design 63, 86

Preliminary Design Review
   milestone 12, 79
premature patternization 35
primitiveness 103
problem domain 15
problem space 4, 5, 17, 74, 81, 89, 103
problem statement 17
process
   as road map 10
   milestones 10
   requirements 10
process specification 126
project management 137
project staffing 136
proof of concept 41
prototype 66
prototyping 41

R

rapid prototyping 41
Rational Rose
   adding operations 101
   and code 139
   equivalence of methods and messages 96
   example model xvii
   excerpts from sample scripts 92, 102, 144, 146
   linking files to use cases 44
   property file excerpt 128
   Requirements tab 128
   starting sequence diagram 85
   writing scripts for sequence diagrams 92
Rational Unified Process (RUP) 2, 63, 130
Rawsthorne, Dan 94
reengineering 27, 40, 45
requirement
   allocating to use cases 129
   allocation 126
   and classes 17
   as named entity 123
   defined 57, 122

requirement, *continued*
  examples 124
  for example system 18
  traceability 126
  types 122
  vs. use case 57
Requirements Review milestone 11, 58
response for a class 143
Responsibility-Driven Design 94
responsibility-driven philosophy 4, 83
reusability 10, 96, 103
reuse 17, 40, 49, 65, 67, 137
reviewability 64, 89
robustness analysis
  and reuse 65
  defined 61
  finishing 78
  key roles 63
  performing 67
robustness diagram
  as checklist 94
  converting to sequence diagram 92
  examples 72, 73
  guiding principles 68
  notation 68
  rules 69
  what not to do 76
Rumbaugh, Jim xvi, 1, 3, 4, 5, 6, 7, 16,
    17, 110, 157, 158

S

scenario 40
scenario-based methods 3, 4
schizophrenic objects 94
science fiction 41
scripts 92, 102, 144, 146
self-aggregation 26
sequence diagram
  and detailed design 64
  and requirements 129
  and robustness analysis 65
  building 85
  defined 84
  elements 84, 85
  examples 141

personnel 136
starting 88
top 10 list 107
versus robustness diagram 65
what not to do 85
Shakespeare, William 8, 158
Shlaer-Mellor method 3
skeleton 33
software blueprint 103
solution space 4, 5, 74, 89, 103
Stahl, Leslie Hulet 123, 157
state diagram
  and requirements 129
  and testing 142
  defined 113
  example 115
  hierarchies 114
  notation 113
  what not to do 110, 114
  when to use 109
state machine 114
state-based testing 142
state-machine-itis 114
state-transition diagram 3
static model
  and requirements 15, 129
  relationship with dynamic model
    83
  updating 74, 100, 138
stereotype 49, 50, 63
stimuli 83
structural methods 3
structured analysis and design 3, 116
subclass 21
sufficiency 103
sunny day scenario 47
superclass 21
swimlanes 116
synchronous message type 111
system boundary 92
system boundary symbol 92

T

technical writers 45, 53, 136
test requirements 122

testing
   black-box 142
   state-based 142
   white-box 142
three amigos xvi, xviii, 1, 2, 5, 9, 62, 63
throwaway diagrams 66
timeout message type 111
top 10 lists 35, 57, 107, 119, 133, 148
traceability 7, 111, 122, 130
true believers 155

U

use case
   and requirements 129
   and testing 142
   defined 38
   example text 42, 46, 51, 52, 53, 54, 55
   factoring out commonality 49, 52, 93
   functional decomposition 117
   identifying 41, 45
   notation 39
   on sequence diagram 84, 86
   peer review 74
   personnel 136
   refining 46, 63
   template 48, 51
   text as contractual agreement 87
   types 40
   vs. requirement 57, 123
   writing 40
use case diagram
   defined 39
   examples 39, 52, 55, 124
   notation 39
   stereotypes 49, 50
   vs. data flow diagram 117

use case driven 2, 41, 103, 142, 146
use case driver 38
use case model
   and reengineering 45
   and user manual 117
   as conceptual center 38
   defined 37
   finishing 57
   purpose 39
   what not to do 49
user acceptance testing 142
user manual 41, 44, 45, 53, 55, 117, 131, 153, 154
uses relationship 149, 150, 152, 155
uses vs. extends 50, 149

V

Van Horn, Brooks 144
Vlissides, John 104, 157

W

weighted methods per class 143
what vs. how 62, 86
white-box testing 142
windows navigation diagram
   defined 43
   elements 43
   example 43
Wirfs-Brock, Rebecca 4, 83, 94, 104, 136, 158

Z

Zembowicz, Robert 102

Object Solutions
Managing the Object-Oriented Project
Grady Booch
Addison-Wesley Object Technology Series

Object Solutions is a direct outgrowth of Grady Booch's experience with object-oriented projects in development around the world. This book focuses on the development process, and is the perfect resource for developers and managers who want to implement object technologies for the first time or refine their existing object-oriented development practice. Drawing upon his knowledge of strategies used in both successful and unsuccessful projects, the author offers pragmatic advice for applying object technologies and controlling projects effectively.

0-8053-0594-7 • Paperback • 336 pages • ©1996

The Unified Modeling Language User Guide
Grady Booch, Ivar Jacobson, and James Rumbaugh
Addison-Wesley Object Technology Series

The Unified Modeling Language User Guide is a two-color introduction to the core eighty percent of the Unified Modeling Language, approaching it in a layered fashion and showing the application of the UML to modeling problems across a wide variety of application domains. This landmark book is suitable for developers unfamiliar with the UML or modeling in general, and will also be useful to experienced developers who wish to learn how to apply the UML to advanced problems.

0-201-57168-4 • Hardcover • 512 pages • ©1999

Surviving Object-Oriented Projects
A Manager's Guide
Alistair Cockburn
Addison-Wesley Object Technology Series

This book allows you to survive, and ultimately succeed with, an object-oriented project. Alistair Cockburn draws on his personal experience and extensive knowledge to provide the information that managers need to combat the unforeseen challenges that await them during project implementation. *Surviving Object-Oriented Projects* supports its key points through short case studies taken from real object-oriented projects. An appendix collects these guidelines and solutions into brief "crib sheets"—ideal for handy reference.

0-201-49834-0 • Paperback • 272 pages • ©1998

Real-Time UML
Developing Efficient Objects for Embedded Systems
Bruce Powel Douglass
Addison-Wesley Object Technology Series

The Unified Modeling Language is particularly suited to modeling real-time and embedded systems. *Real-Time UML* is the introduction that developers of real-time systems need to make the transition to object-oriented analysis and design with UML. The book covers the important features of the UML, and shows how to effectively use these features to model real-time systems. Special in-depth discussions of finite state machines, object identification strategies, and real-time design patterns to help beginning and experienced developers alike are also included.

0-201-32579-9 • Paperback • 400 pages • ©1998

Analysis Patterns
Reusable Object Models
Martin Fowler
Addison-Wesley Object Technology Series

Martin Fowler shares with you his wealth of object modeling experience and his keen eye for solving repeating problems and transforming the solutions into reusable models. *Analysis Patterns* provides a catalog of patterns that have emerged in a wide range of domains, including trading, measurement, accounting, and organizational relationships.

0-201-89542-0 • Hardcover • 384 pages • ©1997

UML Distilled
Applying the Standard Object Modeling Language
Martin Fowler with Kendall Scott
Foreword by Grady Booch, Ivar Jacobson, and James Rumbaugh
Addison-Wesley Object Technology Series

Recipient of *Software Development* magazine's 1997 Productivity Award, this concise overview introduces you to the Unified Modeling Language, highlighting the key elements of its notation, semantics, and processes. Included is a brief explanation of UML's history, development, and rationale, as well as discussions on how UML can be integrated into the object-oriented development process. The book also profiles various modeling techniques associated with UML—use cases, CRC cards, design by contract, dynamic classification, interfaces, and abstract classes.

0-201-32563-2 • Paperback • 208 pages • ©1997

Software Reuse

Architecture, Process, and Organization for Business Success
Ivar Jacobson, Martin Griss, and Patrik Jonsson
Addison-Wesley Object Technology Series

This book brings software engineers, designers, programmers, and their managers a giant step closer to a future in which object-oriented component-based software engineering is the norm. Jacobson, Griss, and Jonsson develop a coherent model and set of guidelines for ensuring success with large-scale, systematic, object-oriented reuse. Their framework, referred to as "Reuse-Driven Software Engineering Business" (Reuse Business) deals systematically with the key business process, architecture, and organization issues that hinder success with reuse.

0-201-92476-5 • Hardcover • 560 pages • ©1997

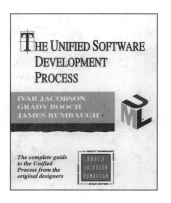

The Unified Software Development Process

Ivar Jacobson, Grady Booch, and James Rumbaugh
Addison-Wesley Object Technology Series

The Unified Software Development Process goes beyond other object-oriented analysis and design methods by detailing a family of processes that incorporate the complete lifecycle of software development. This new book, representing the collaboration of Ivar Jacobson, Grady Booch, and James Rumbaugh, clearly describes the different higher-level constructs—notation as well as semantics—used in the models. Thus stereotypes such as use cases and actors, packages, classes, interfaces, active classes, processes and threads, nodes, and most relations are described intuitively in the context of a model.

0-201-57169-2 • Hardcover • 512 pages • ©1999

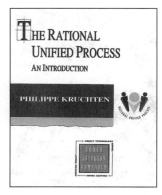

The Rational Unified Process

An Introduction
Philippe Kruchten
Addison-Wesley Object Technology Series

This concise book offers a quick introduction to the concepts, structure, content, and motivation of the Rational Unified Process. This revolutionary software development process provides a disciplined approach to assigning, managing, and completing tasks within a software development organization and is the first development process to exploit the full capabilities of the industry-standard Unified Modeling Language. *The Rational Unified Process* is unique in that it captures many of the proven best practices in modern software development and presents them in a form that can be tailored to a wide range of projects and organizations.

0-201-60459-0 • Paperback • 272 pages • ©1999

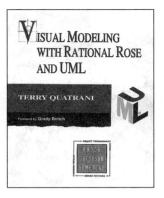

Visual Modeling with Rational Rose and UML

Terry Quatrani

Addison-Wesley Object Technology Series

Terry Quatrani, the Rose Evangelist for Rational Software Corporation, teaches you visual modeling and the UML, enabling you to apply an iterative and incremental process to analysis and design. With the practical direction offered in this book, you will be able to specify, visualize, document, and create software solutions. Highlights of this book include an examination of system behavior from a use case approach; a discussion of the concepts and notations used for finding objects and classes; an introduction to the notation needed to create and document a system's architecture; and a review of the iteration planning process.

0-201-31016-3 • Paperback • 240 pages • ©1998

Software Project Management

A Unified Framework
Walker Royce
Foreword by Barry Boehm
Addison-Wesley Object Technology Series

This book presents a new management framework uniquely suited to the complexities of modern software development. Walker Royce's pragmatic perspective exposes the shortcomings of many well-accepted management priorities and equips software professionals with state-of-the-art knowledge derived from his twenty years of successful from-the-trenches management experience. In short, the book provides the software industry with field-proven benchmarks for making tactical decisions and strategic choices that will enhance an organization's probability of success.

0-201-30958-0 • Hardcover • 448 pages • ©1998

The Unified Modeling Language Reference Manual

James Rumbaugh, Ivar Jacobson, and Grady Booch
Addison-Wesley Object Technology Series

James Rumbaugh, Ivar Jacobson, and Grady Booch have created the definitive reference to the UML. This two-color book covers every aspect and detail of the UML and presents the modeling language in a useful reference format that serious software architects or programmers should have on their bookshelf. The book is organized by topic and designed for quick access. The authors also provide the necessary information to enable existing OMT, Booch, and OOSE notation users to make the transition to UML. The book provides an overview of the semantic foundation of the UML through a concise appendix.

0-201-30998-X • Hardcover with CD-ROM • 576 pages • ©1999

Applying Use Cases
A Practical Guide
Geri Schneider and Jason P. Winters
Addison-Wesley Object Technology Series

Applying Use Cases provides a practical and clear introduction to developing use cases, demonstrating their use via a continuing case study. Using the Unified Software Development Process as a framework and the Unified Modeling Language as a notation, the authors step the reader through applying use cases in the different phases of the process, focusing on where and how use cases are best applied. The book also offers insight into the common mistakes and pitfalls that can plague an object-oriented project.

0-201-30981-5 • Paperback • 208 pages • ©1998

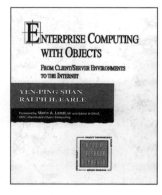

Enterprise Computing with Objects
From Client/Server Environments to the Internet
Yen-Ping Shan and Ralph H. Earle
Addison-Wesley Object Technology Series

This book helps you place rapidly evolving technologies—such as the Internet, the World Wide Web, distributed computing, object technology, and client/server systems—in their appropriate contexts when preparing for the development, deployment, and maintenance of information systems. The authors distinguish what is essential from what is incidental, while imparting a clear understanding of how the underlying technologies fit together. The book examines essential topics, including data persistence, security, performance, scalability, and development tools.

0-201-32566-7 • Paperback • 448 pages • ©1998

The Object Constraint Language
Precise Modeling with UML
Jos Warmer and Anneke Kleppe
Addison-Wesley Object Technology Series

The Object Constraint Language is a new notational language, a subset of the Unified Modeling Language, that allows software developers to express a set of rules that govern very specific aspects of an object in object-oriented applications. With the OCL, developers are able to more easily express unique limitations and write the fine print that is often necessary in complex software designs. The authors' pragmatic approach and illustrative use of examples will help application developers to quickly get up to speed.

0-201-37940-6 • Paperback • 144 pages • ©1999

Addison-Wesley Computer and Engineering Publishing Group

How to Interact with Us

1. Visit our Web site

http://www.awl.com/cseng

When you think you've read enough, there's always more content for you at Addison-Wesley's web site. Our web site contains a directory of complete product information including:

- Chapters
- Exclusive author interviews
- Links to authors' pages
- Tables of contents
- Source code

You can also discover what tradeshows and conferences Addison-Wesley will be attending, read what others are saying about our titles, and find out where and when you can meet our authors and have them sign your book.

2. Subscribe to Our Email Mailing Lists

Subscribe to our electronic mailing lists and be the first to know when new books are publishing. Here's how it works: Sign up for our electronic mailing at **http://www.awl.com/cseng/mailinglists.html**. Just select the subject areas that interest you and you will receive notification via email when we publish a book in that area.

3. Contact Us via Email

cepubprof@awl.com
Ask general questions about our books.
Sign up for our electronic mailing lists.
Submit corrections for our web site.

bexpress@awl.com
Request an Addison-Wesley catalog.
Get answers to questions regarding your order or our products.

innovations@awl.com
Request a current Innovations Newsletter.

webmaster@awl.com
Send comments about our web site.

jcs@awl.com
Submit a book proposal.
Send errata for an Addison-Wesley book.

cepubpublicity@awl.com
Request a review copy for a member of the media interested in reviewing new Addison-Wesley titles.

We encourage you to patronize the many fine retailers who stock Addison-Wesley titles. Visit our online directory to find stores near you or visit our online store: **http://store.awl.com/** or call **800-824-7799**.

Addison Wesley Longman
Computer and Engineering Publishing Group
One Jacob Way, Reading, Massachusetts 01867 USA
TEL 781-944-3700 • FAX 781-942-3076

When you're ready to apply *Use Case Driven Object Modeling*, check out the *Rose 98 for Power Users* CD by Doug Rosenberg.

In this state-of-the-art multimedia tutorial, ICONIX President Doug Rosenberg will teach you how to optimize your project's usage of Rational Rose 98 in support of a use case driven UML modeling process. Topics include an introduction to use case driven object modeling, scripting, how to load custom stereotypes into Rose, and a variety of productivity tips for using Rose more efficiently. The CD also introduces the Objectory stereotypes for boundary, control, and entity objects and explains why they will help your UML modeling efforts.

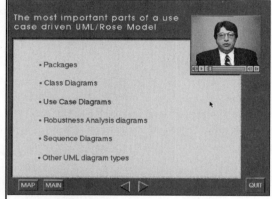

The tutorial includes 20 narrated example movies of Rose 98, including:
• Installing the Objectory Add-In
• Linking Screen Pictures to Use Case Specifications
• A script that automatically starts a Sequence Diagram
• Custom Properties to support Requirements Traceability
• Allocating Classes to Components for Code Generation
• Automatically export models from Rose into MS Word
• Using OLE Automation to export from Rose to MS Excel
• Guided tour of the Rose Extensibility Interface (REI)

You'll learn:
• The key elements of a use case driven UML model.
• How to tailor Rose to your project's specific needs.
• How to use OLE automation from your scripts.
• The scripting tutorial introduces the Rose Extensibility Interface (REI), which defines the programmatic interface to Rose. A Rose model presenting the REI classes is provided on the CD for reference.

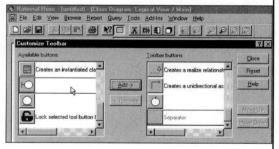

A collection of useful scripts is included, along with the Objectory add-in and a 30-day evaluation copy of Rose 98.

Available at an easily affordable price of only $99, or included at no extra charge as part of the ICONIX Unified Object Modeling CD-ROM tutorial set, "Rose 98 for Power Users" is guaranteed to improve your productivity when doing use case driven UML modeling with Rational Rose.

ORDER ONLINE AT:http://www.iconixsw.com/Rose98CD.html

ICONIX Software Engineering, Inc.
2800 28th Street, Suite 320 Santa Monica, CA 90405
Email: sales@iconixsw.com / Phone: 310-458-0092 / Fax: 310-396-3454

SPECIAL OFFER!!! Mention "Use Case Driven Object Modeling with UML"
when ordering online, and take 10% off the price of any ICONIX multimedia tutorial !

http://www.iconixsw.com